In Pursuit of Color

In Pursuit of Color

From fungi to fossil fuels: uncovering the origins of the world's most famous dyes.

atelier éditions | d·a·p

↑ Dyer's yarn hangs above an alley
in the Moroccan city of Fes, 1964

Contents

Introduction

IN THE SUMMER OF 2017, a 36-second video clip turned a pack of stray dogs into an internet sensation. One of the dogs lopes across a road, staring down the camera; another mutt follows, hopping on three legs. But it's not your average internet pet video. The dogs aren't skateboarding or snuggling with baby goats. Instead, they're blue. Seeking refuge from Mumbai's sweltering heat, the pack had gone for a swim in the city's Kasadi river. When they emerged, their fur (previously mottled mixes of golden-retriever blond, alsatian gray, and pound-puppy brown) had turned shades ranging from pale baby blue to vivid turquoise. One dog had deep navy spots.

Arati Chauhan, a local animal rights activist, filmed the scene and posted it on her social media. The blue dogs were picked up by international news sites including the *Guardian*, the BBC, and *National Geographic*. Animal rights activists filled comments sections with indignation, and the clip eventually caught the attention of Berlin-based graphic designer Patrick Thomas (who was my own introduction to the so-called "smurf dog" video). His curiosity piqued by the strays, Thomas was determined to find out how they'd become blue.

In his efforts, Thomas traced the blue dye in the river back to its likely source. The canines' swimming spot was downstream from Ducol Organics, a paint and plastics factory that allegedly released its untreated liquid waste into the river. He contacted Ducol repeatedly but to no avail, though his research into the dye itself proved more productive. The dye that had turned the dogs blue was indigo: the same substance used to make Chairman Mao's iconic suits, James Dean's jeans, Napoleon's uniforms, and King Tutankhamun's burial shrouds. It was this substance—the world's primary blue dye—that led me to an air-conditioned auditorium at London's Victoria and Albert Museum in late 2021. I settled into my seat for a panel talk on indigo, where I heard Thomas speak with two co-hosts: fellow designer Tony Brook, who had also been entranced by the mysterious blue canines, and indigo scholar Dr Jenny Balfour-Paul.

In the four years since the blue mutts first ambled across his screen, Thomas had become indigo-obsessed. A quick google to find the source of the dogs' smurfiness had turned into a quest that has spanned continents. And Thomas isn't the only one intrigued by the materials that make color. I was sitting in the audience that day because I had fallen down the rabbit hole a few years before; a casual interest in natural dyeing had turned into the obsession that eventually led to this book.

The word "dye" evolved from its Old English root, *dēag*, or *dēah*, meaning color, though "dye" now refers to something more specific. A dye is a substance that changes the color of the material it's applied to, including fibers, yarns, fabrics, paper, leather, wood—or dog hair—by forming a chemical bond with that material. Like Thomas's puzzlement over the blue dogs, most of us don't know how things are dyed, and we tend to think about the textiles around us least of all (they lack the novelty and shock value of a navy canine). While textiles surround us almost every moment of our lives—from the crisp cotton sheets we tuck ourselves into at night to the uniforms we don for our daily work, and the train and car seats we ride on to get there—they're so ubiquitous that we usually overlook them.

Like textiles, dyes are everywhere, speaking to us in ways we take for granted. When we see a person dressed in teal-green scrubs we know they're likely a nurse or doctor; while police uniforms are so strongly associated with the color navy that cops are often referred to as the "boys in blue." We have a cultural understanding of what colors mean, whether it's on our clothes, in the decor of our homes, or out in the streets. But most of us don't know how our plump sofa cushions were made green, or why our jeans turn that perfect shade of faded blue.

There are a few reasons for this disconnect. For one thing, textile and clothing production usually happens far away from the end-consumer. As a result, the work involved in making our favorite outfits—mining, growing, harvesting, cleaning, weaving, knitting, sewing, and dyeing—is invisible to most people who purchase the final products. Second, almost all dyes and over half of the clothes produced each year are synthetics made from fossil fuels, and imagining how gloopy black oil is transformed into a pile of fluffy pink sweaters is pretty mind-boggling.

We weren't always so cut off from the sources of color. For most of human history, the dyestuffs, or the raw materials that made dyes, were some of the most valuable and contentious commodities in the world. Indigo alone has been the cause of political uprisings, trade wars, and fear-mongering propaganda. As recently as 150 years ago most people would have had some familiarity with the materials that make dyes, even if they couldn't afford them. We've lost a hard-won literacy of color that was earned over millennia of experimentation and research. Reclaiming this knowledge isn't just about understanding the past, it might be one of the ways we can address many of the social and environmental issues that face us today.

Understanding what's involved in producing the textiles around us might also equip us to make more-informed decisions for ourselves and our planet. According to one estimate, the textile and leather industries dump 625,000 tons of chemicals—or about 250 Olympic swimming pools' worth of toxic sludge—into our water supplies each year. Much of this is heavy metals and colorants from the dyeing process, and the untreated wastewater from dye factories can be so caustic that it causes instant chemical burns on human skin. Chemicals common in the run-off, like aromatic amines, are known poisons that kill aquatic life and increase the incidence of cancer and other illnesses in humans.

Water aside, if we can better understand the enormous volume of resources and labor that go into making the textiles we use, we might start to value them differently (and maybe even hold onto them a bit longer). According to one 2018 estimate, as much as 5 percent of all the space in landfills is taken up by clothing and other textiles. The equivalent of one garbage truck full of clothes is incinerated or buried in landfills every second. Dunes of brightly colored clothing (comprising both second-hand and unsold production from some of the world's most well-known brands) form an informal graveyard in Chile's Atacama Desert, while rainbow swathes of second-hand clothes now regularly wash onto Ghana's once-pristine beaches. The mountains of hardly used clothes dumped around the world are a shockingly visible sign of the disposability with which many regard their wardrobes.

This book is an effort to reconnect the fluffy pink sweaters to the raw materials and processes that make them. *In Pursuit of Color* focuses especially on dyes and textiles; in recent years, there's been a proliferation of excellent books on the history of color in art and more broadly, but I felt there was a space left to fill with the stories of dyes.

The difference between color in art history and color in textile history largely comes down to dyes versus pigments—two words that are often used interchangeably but are distinct. The main difference is their molecular size, which affects how they behave chemically. Compared with pigments, dyes are tiny molecules, a trait that makes them soluble, meaning the minuscule dye molecules dissolve in the medium into which they are mixed (most often this is water, sometimes ammonia, and sometimes a heady mix of weirder stuff) and then re-form, bonding with the fibers in the pot at a molecular level.

Though sometimes getting dyes to dissolve can be hard work—requiring multiple chemical reactions, additives like ammonia and calcium carbonate (lime), and pH modifiers like vinegar—the comparatively mammoth pigment molecules don't dissolve at all. Instead, pigments are suspended in the medium, which means they don't form chemical bonds with the material they are coloring, they sit on top of it. Dyes are *in* the cloth, pigments (in the form of printing inks, paints, etc.) are *on* it.

Chemically, pigments can be either organic or inorganic compounds, whereas dyes are always the former. Organic compounds contain atoms of carbon that are covalently bonded to atoms of other elements, usually hydrogen, nitrogen, or oxygen (meaning they share electrons with them, creating some of the strongest molecular connections in nature). Practically speaking, this means more materials work as pigments than dyes—aspiring painters have used everything from white lead to Egyptian mummies on their canvases. Savvy color-makers can even turn dyes into pigments (usually called lake pigments) through a series of chemical manipulations that bump up their molecular bulk.

There are a lot of technical snippets like this, and as the materials and techniques used in dyeing aren't widely known, the book begins with a brief introduction to its technical side, showcasing the substances that have played supporting roles in the epic story of dyeing in *Metals That Bite*, *Astringent Color*, and *The Invisible Ingredient*. A brief history of dyeing in the West follows, providing context for the social, geographic, and political landscapes discussed throughout this book.

Then some of the world's most-loved dyes are split across four sections —*Flora*, *Fauna*, *Fungi*, and *Fossil Fuels*—separated by material pedigree. The first three parts focus on the plants, animals, mushrooms, and lichens that were responsible for all dyes before the commercial success of synthetic dyes in the late 19th century. These stories track the extreme (and sometimes bizarre) lengths that humans have gone to to make our lives more colorful: be it plucking out the snotty glands of a carnivorous sea snail to make history's most valuable purple, or ferrying insect-infested cacti across mountains to protect a vulnerable source of scarlet. Famous historical color recipes are set alongside the stories, illustrating just how dirty humans have been willing to get to produce bright, permanent dyes (think fermenting your own urine, mixing it with goat blood and patiently waiting a month for the mixture to mature). The recipes have been modernized for readability but historical measurements and ingredients have been left mostly intact.

The last section of the book, *Fossil Fuels*, picks up in the mid-19th century with the invention of the first commercially successful synthetic dye, mauveine. The subsequent race to make new synthetic colors led to the natural dye industry's demise, and brought on a chemical revolution that led to the creation of the modern pharmaceutical industry.

Fossil Fuels is all about the synthetic. It's a term often used in opposition to *natural* (a word with nine dictionary definitions that's been co-opted for a sweeping range of marketing slogans and political agendas), and as a result its meaning is a bit slippery. For our purpose, "synthetic" refers to dyes that are derived from the by-products of fossil fuels—non-renewable resources made from the remains of prehistoric plant matter—that have been synthesized, which refers to what happens when simple(ish) compounds are joined together to make a more complicated one. In contrast, natural dyes are derived from renewable sources like plants, bugs, and mushrooms.

One could argue—and people do—that the nature/synthetic binary doesn't make sense. Fossil fuels occur naturally, without human intervention, while many of the plants and animals that have historically provided us with "natural" dyes wouldn't exist in their current form without selective breeding and other human meddling.

Interdisciplinary designer Charlotte McCurdy, for example, has argued for categorizing all forms of energy as either the product of "ancient sunlight" or "present-tense sunlight." And she has a point. But the terms "synthetic" and "natural" are so embedded in English usage that it's hard to talk about dyes in any other way. Following McCurdy's lead, I chose to lay the stories of famous synthetic dyes alongside natural ones to try to level the material playing field. I'm interested in the lives of the dyes before they get into our clothes—as well as after—and categorizing the dyes by source made more sense to me than separating them out by color.

To tackle any leftover linguistic and technical questions, the booklet of this set is designed to help you with the terminology, provide a practical guide to the dyeing process, and encourage you to try some dyeing yourself. While commonly used terms will be explained throughout the book, if you're eager to know more about *copperas*, *orpiment*, or *luteolin*, dip in and out of the glossary in the appendices booklet, Dyeing Principles and Procedures, that can be found in the back of the book.

I started this project intending to write a global survey of dyes, but early on in my research I realized the stories that were available were skewed. I had bitten off more than I could chew. To start, most of the surviving information about prehistoric dyeing is concentrated on practices from the Mediterranean regions of what is now North Africa and Southern Europe. Further, surviving written sources about dyes from the Medieval Era through to the Industrial Revolution are most often European, taking the form of dye manuals for domestic and industrial use (with the latter often connected to colonial expansion). There are also limits to my own knowledge; as a Canadian who has been based in London, UK, for the last decade, my research has been influenced and limited by the places I have lived and the sources to which I've had access. *In Pursuit of Color* is not a complete history of dyeing; instead these volumes introduce some of the most culturally salient and economically important materials that humans have ever forgotten about.

On *Scientific Names*

After hearing about Oregon grape, a shrub in the barberry family that creates an acid yellow dye, during a chat with a Canadian dyer, I typed the plant's name into my search engine. I quickly realized that we in the UK call it mahonia, and that I have one nestled amongst two plum trees in my back garden.

In order to give you the best chance of a similar revelation, scientific names are used alongside common names for species to help you recognize and find the dyes mentioned in this book. Hopefully it's useful, but it should be said that scientific naming isn't a system without faults. For one, Western science has a long colonial history that continues to involve giving names to plants that ignore their existing ones and their local histories. In 2022, a tree discovered in the Ebo forest in Cameroon was named *Uvariopsis dicaprio* after the actor Leonardo Dicaprio, in honor of his conservation funding but ignoring the contributions of the local Banen communities and Cameroonian researchers who have long campaigned to protect the forest and its biodiversity.

Second, scientific names are in a state of flux. The Linnaean system of Latin names for plants and animals is based on appearance: those with the same features are considered to be related, and this relationship is indicated by a hierarchy of names going from the most basic (kingdom, e.g. plant or animal) to the fine grained (at the bottom are family and then genus, within which are species). Species names are called binomials, and are made up of the genus followed by the species: woad, for example, is in the family Brassicaceae (the mustards), and the genus *Isatis* (a group of about 80 flowering plants), so its Latin name or binomial is *Isatis tinctoria*. However, the names aren't fixed, as scientists constantly review these relationships and make new discoveries. DNA analysis in particular has had a large impact in the 21st century, allowing living organisms to be examined at the molecular level: species once thought to be closely related can be found to be genetically very different. One example is brazilwood: given the name *Caesalpinia echinata* in 1785, recent gene studies showed it was so different from other species of *Caesalpinia* that a new genus was needed, and it was renamed *Paubrasilia echinata* in 2016.

Dyeing—
The Essentials

UNCLOTHED, THE HUMAN BODY is remarkably sensitive to its surroundings, prone to feeling chilly if the temperature drops just a few degrees (not to mention blistering sunburns or itching bug bites). For millennia, textiles have provided protection, warmth, and shelter, too. From the yurt, a circular tent used by nomadic people in central Asia from at least 600 BCE to the nylon pop-up tent pitched for a weekend camping trip, we've come to rely on fabric to make spaces for us to eat, sleep, be social, and keep the elements at bay. But while textiles fulfill a whole host of functional needs, the same cannot be said for the dyes that color them. According to anthropologists, dyes are only about human desire.

The reasons for dyeing are thought to be purely social: colorful clothing has been used to distinguish, ostracize, celebrate, and mourn since time immemorial. Yellow, for example, symbolized joy, fertility, and prosperity during the Roman Republic (*c.*509–27 BCE), and was worn at weddings by the betrothed couple, who would enter a ceremonial room painted the same hue. The ubiquitous white wedding dress is a trend originated by Queen Victoria and made more popular by the invention of photography; light-colored dresses look comparatively sharp in sepia-tone prints.

During the Edo period in Japan (1603–1868), strict hierarchical laws governed what colors and fabrics could be worn by everyone in society (the laws even extended to puppets). More than a few societies have required certain groups of people to wear visible, colorful badges that have, at times, been used to indicate religious difference, or demarcate professions ranging from executioners and minstrels to beggars and hairdressers. Sex work tops the list as the most frequently targeted profession. At various times over the centuries sex workers have been required to wear a red dress, a yellow badge, cloaks ranging from white to black to canary yellow, and, most recently, a fluorescent chartreuse safety vest.

For better or worse, dyes—those colored substances that chemically bond with the material they're applied to—have made all that color-coding possible. And the whole (rather long) process starts with dyestuffs, the raw materials that are processed into dyes. For most of human history, dyestuffs have been natural materials that look a lot like garden waste; a bit of bark here, a few dried-up bugs there, a gnarled root or two. These materials have one thing in common: they either contain *colorants*, which are the compounds that bring the color to the dye pot, or *precursors*, substances that need to be chemically transformed into colorants before they can be used. Each colorant can dye a range of shades depending on its concentration, the mordants used (we'll get to those shortly), the type of fiber being dyed, and even the water.

Regardless of the scale they're used at (or the end purpose), dyestuffs need to be processed into dyes, a step that ranges from a simple task like chopping them up and tossing the dyestuffs into a pot of hot water, to a complicated undertaking that involves multiple rounds of chemical manipulation, months of waiting, and supplemental ingredients that include everything from animal bones to wheat bran to urine.

After processing the dyestuff, the soon-to-be dyed material needs to be pre-treated. In this book, the materials dyed are mostly natural fibers that come from plants and animals, and the textiles (also called cloth or fabric) that they are spun and woven into, a niche chosen for two reasons. First, like natural dyes, natural fibers made up all the textiles in the world until less than a century ago; the first commercial synthetic fiber was nylon, patented in 1938. Second, natural dyes don't dye synthetic fibers. So the plant, animal, and fungi dyes that make up most of this book haven't had much interaction with synthetics like polyester or acrylic.

Natural fibers are split into two primary categories based on their chemical makeup: protein and cellulose. Protein fibers are made from animal hair or the shimmering filaments that can be unraveled from a silkworm's cocoon, while cellulose fibers are plant fibers like linen (made from sinewy strings pulled from the stalks of a rotting flax plant) and cotton (plucked from a fluffy boll that protects the seeds of a shrub). Together, protein and cellulose fibers make up most of this book's focus, though there are a few other uses for dye that were too interesting, culturally salient, or just plain weird for this author to pass up—like tracking the sexual partners of ancient Assyrian sheep.

Sheep aside, if you're working with fiber, yarn, or fabric, the next step in the dye process is scouring, which is a rigorous cleaning process that removes any gums, waxes, and dirt lurking in the material. How you proceed from here depends on both the dye and the kind of material you're working with. After scouring, protein fibers, like wool, alpaca, and silk, often need mordanting (cellulose fibers require an extra step first, which we'll get to presently).

↓ European blueprint, a mix of resist block printing and indigo dye, at the H. Fischer dye works in Neukirch/Lausitz, Germany, 1940

Metals That *Bite*

16

FROM THE LATIN *MORDERE*, "to bite," mordants are (usually) metal salts that bind dye molecules to fibers. There are some exceptions, but most natural dyes require mordants to be lightfast and washfast, which means that the fabric won't fade when it's exposed to sunlight or thrown in a washing machine. Despite their widespread application over millennia, the chemical nuances of mordanting processes are not completely understood because of the sprawling variety of dyes and the wide range of materials that they're used on.

We know that mordants form molecular bonds between the fiber and the dye molecules, but the bonds themselves differ depending on the dyestuff's colorants and the type of fibers being dyed. Natural dyes often contain multiple colorants, too, so it's not always clear which molecules are sticking to which, and the exact nature of every mordant/dye/fabric relationship is yet to be determined.

A handful of compounds work as mordants. Alum, a compound of aluminum sulfate and another sulfate—most commonly aluminum potassium sulfate and aluminum acetate—is the most prevalent, historically important, and least toxic. It brightens the color of fabric and improves the permanence of dye.

Alum is usually found as a mineral, either in relatively pure form as a clear crystal, or as part of a shale from which it's extracted. There are also plant species that hyper-accumulate aluminum (sucking it up from the surrounding soil and storing it in their leaves) and dyers make use of these plant-mordants too. The most well-known are species of *Symplocos*, a leafy shrub.

Mordanting with alum is relatively simple; you calculate how much you need in proportion to the weight of fiber that you're dyeing, and dissolve that amount in a pot of hot water. Then you add your fiber. You wait for a while, then take the fiber out. Depending on the dye and fiber there can be some variation, but that's basically it. This simple process makes a huge difference to the permanence of dyes, which is why alum has been prized since antiquity.

The earliest textile evidence of alum use is a patterned cloth of powder-blue and pink stripes with a little blue fringe, found at the Egyptian pyramid of Unas, and woven around 2350 BCE. In the three millennia that followed, alum became an immensely valuable commodity. A 16th-century Venetian handbook on metalworking, *De la Pirotechnia*, sums up just how essential it was: "nor could dyers of cloth and wool work without it, for alum is as necessary to them as bread to men."

In 1678, Daniel Colwall, a founding member of the Royal Society in Britain, published an essay on the burgeoning Yorkshire alum industry, "An Account of the English Alum-Works," that offers insight into the arduous extraction of purified alum from the dark rocky shale quarried from the northern English county for centuries. (Colwall is now better remembered as a merchant and philanthropist than as a scientist—his other contributions to chemistry include a paper entitled "Ordering Oysters at Colchester".)

When Colwall published his account, the English alum industry was on its way to becoming a chemical giant. Its growth had started more than a century earlier, during the latter years of the rule of Henry VIII, because of the political turmoil caused by the first of the king's divorces. During Henry's reign the European alum industry was a monopoly controlled by the pope. When Henry divorced his Catholic wife, Catherine of Aragon, and set himself up as the head of a separate English Church, the country's access to alum was suddenly dependent on an unsympathetic foreign power. Since England had a colossal wool trade that relied heavily on the availability of alum as a mordant for dyeing, this was a painful economic blow.

Two cousins—both named Thomas Chaloner—were the ones to jumpstart the English alum industry. One Thomas was a courtier with a sprawling estate at Guisborough in Yorkshire, the other had a profound interest in geology. When the latter visited his cousin's Yorkshire estate, he noted that the rock formations were the same as ones he'd seen at alum mines in Italy, and foreseeing the business potential the cousins decided to get into the alum industry together.

But when the Chaloners approached the local townspeople to collect urine, a vital source of ammonia used to process the shale into pure alum, they hit an unexpected snag. To increase the volume to sell, the urine for sale was sometimes bulked up with seawater, and though the dilution was undetectable by sight or smell it rendered the urine useless for alum production. According to Colwall, "If the urine be good, it will work like yeast put to beer or ale, but if mingled it will stir no more ... than water." But despite the occasional urine tampering, the Yorkshire alum industry thrived for over 300 years.

Following alum in economic and cultural importance as a mordant is iron (usually in the form of ferrous sulfate), which darkens and mutes dyes instead of brightening them. Iron's darkening power has made it useful for shifting pale yellows to khaki greens, pinks to burgundies, and, most famously, making dark grays and inky blacks. It shows up in historical recipes as copperas or green vitriol, and in this book, is a crucial ingredient in the story of logwood (see page 66)—a spindly tree whose inner heartwood possesses a bluish purple dye that was used with iron to make sumptuous black fabrics. Today, ferrous sulfate can be bought as purified crystals, but craft dyers often make their own by adding bits of rusty metal to a solution of vinegar and water.

Unlike alum, dyers don't always use iron to pre-soak their fabrics before dyeing; instead, it's sometimes used as an after-bath or even painted directly onto fabrics as a kind of resist. A well-known example of the latter process is a cotton textile from Mali called bogolan or bogolanfini, or, aptly, mud cloth. As anyone who has ever slipped down a muddy hill on a rainy day knows, mud is very good at staining clothes, and this is especially true when it contains iron, so dyers have long used iron-rich soils to make powerful, black-brown hues.

Bogolanfini was internationally popularized by fashion designer Chris Seydou (born Seydou Nourou Doumbia). Seydou grew up in Mali and

↗ Children grinding n'galaman and n'tjankara plants to create yellow dye for the bogolanfini process in Bamako, Mali, 1969

→ Ground n'galaman and n'tjankara plants for yellow dye, bogolanfini process, Bamako, Mali, 1969

↓ Boubacar Doumbia (Groupe Kasobane), director of NDOMO, the conservatory center for natural dyeing techniques, explaining the ancient symbols of a traditional bogolanfini, Ségou, Mali, 2020

in 1972 at the age of 22 moved to Paris to pursue a career in fashion. In 1980, after nearly a decade working for the likes of Yves Saint Laurent and Paco Rabanne, Seydou returned to his homeland and turned his focus to bogolan, a fabric traditionally used for ritual functions by rural communities. Seydou looked to bogolan to create a distinct esthetic, commissioning his own versions of the patterns and isolating motifs from their surroundings, applying them to Western cuts and silhouettes and bringing them to the runway.

To make bogolanfini, a dye bath is prepared with the tannin-rich leaves of the n'galama (*Anogeissus leiocarpa*), a tall deciduous tree native to Africa's savannas. Then, the fabric is soaked in the dye water, and the cloth, now buttery yellow, is pulled out of the bath and dried in the sun. Once dry, artisans paint the fabric. The paint, repeatedly applied in intricate motifs, is fermented mud harvested from the bottom or banks of the Niger river and stored in jars for a year or two before use. The iron-rich earth reacts with the tannins—acting as both mordant and dye—and the final cloths vary in color from warm browns to near blacks. As a final step, a mixture of ground peanuts, millet bran, and caustic soda is used to bleach the yellow background, turning it a bright white. The results are striking, graphic fabrics that have been much imitated, having a wide-reaching influence on African style and the global fashion industry to this day.

Across China and Southeast Asia there is a long history of using a similar method to make so-called "gummed silk" (it has a spate of other names thanks to its widespread popularity and imprecise English translations). Due to the processes used, on one side the silks are a rich brownish-orange, and on the other, deep obsidian.

While iron and alum are the most well-known mordants, tin (stannous chloride), copper (copper sulfate), and chrome (potassium chloride) have been used too, though they are all more toxic than alum and iron and have fallen out of use on a craft scale. The use of copper, called blue vitriol or blue copperas, dates back at least 1,800 years, while chrome wasn't widely used until the 19th century, though it's of huge commercial importance today and used for a range of synthetic dyes despite its toxicity and the polluting waste that it creates.

Astringent *Color*

BEFORE MORDANTING, CELLULOSE fibers, like cotton, linen, and jute, require a tannin step. If you've ever swizzled a glass of red wine, sipped on a hot coffee, or spread some blackberry jam on your toast, you're probably more familiar with tannins than you think (the same goes for green tea, beer, chocolate, mangoes, persimmons, and pomegranates).

Plants use tannins as a defense mechanism. Unripe fruit, for instance, tastes bitter to discourage creatures from eating it and spreading seeds before they're ready. Unfortunately for plants, this has backfired. Humans have developed a taste for tannins—and not just in our morning coffee. We use bitter barks, seeds, and leaves for making color, too.

Tannins are a catch-all group of thousands of astringent compounds called polyphenols. All tannins are big, complicated molecules that bind readily with proteins, starches, cellulose, and minerals—a key attribute when it comes to dyeing.

They're generally split into four families: the first are gallotannins, named after their primary source, oak galls, which are tannin-rich growths found on gall or Aleppo oak trees that have long been used by dyers.

Then there are ellagitannins, proanthocyanidins, and complex tannins. Each contains at least a few dozen molecules and exist in plants around the globe, and some are more effective in the dye vat than others. Even within the same plants, there can be a whole host of different tannins at play. For instance, the galls on Chinese sumac (*Rhus javanica*) are the richest source of gallotannin known and contain numerous tannin varieties.

We have a good idea of the molecular structures of tannins and a decent understanding of how they interact, but it's still not understood how all of their relationships work. Since there are so many, watching how they interact differently with various dyes, fabrics, and mordants is like following the cast of a molecular soap opera.

For our purposes, tannins do three different things in the dye vat. First, they act as a mordant. But unlike the mordants in *Metals That Bite*, which act as connective bridges between fibers and dyes, tannins form insoluble bonds between cellulose fibers like cotton and linen and the mordants themselves, creating brighter, bolder colors that don't wash out. As a result, cellulose fibers are usually soaked in a tannin bath before mordanting.

This tannin-bath step is known as *galling* or *sumaching* because oak galls and sumac are the most common materials used. Oak galls have clear tannins; if you use them to *gall* your cloth and expect to see a color change, you'll be disappointed when you pull your fabric from the dye pot. But if you overdye fabric with another color after a soak in a gall bath, their effect will be immediately clear; your cloth will be brighter, more color-fast, and more even.

Other parts of the oaks have been used too; the tannin-rich bark and acorns have been so critical that they've leant themselves to the etymology. The English word *tannin* is derived from leather tanning, a process that makes raw hides more waterproof and less degradable. *Tanning*, in turn, comes from *tannum*, the Latin for "oak bark," which has given its name to the process because the tree husks were so commonly used to treat hides.

Tannins are also dyes in their own right. Most range from creams to yellows to soft, tawny browns. For example, even though pomegranate rinds and seeds are deep crimson, their tannins are soft greenish yellows. Indian recipes from the Mughal period (1526—1857) use pomegranate

↓ Catechu, also known as Cutch, is a solid extract obtained by evaporating a decoction of the leaves of gambier (*Uncaria gambir*)

on its own, with other tannin-rich plants, or with an iron mordant to make emeralds and bottle greens. Myrobalan, a common tannin plant from India, tints fabric the color of freshly churned butter. A subsequent dip in an indigo vat will give you rich shades of turquoise and aquamarine. The tannins in sumac dye fabrics the fleshy pinks of renaissance paintings. But sumac, a flowering plant that's related to the cashew, has also been layered into russets, oranges, violets, grays, and deep, striking blacks. Alongside oak galls, sumacs are some of the most widely used tannins in dyeing, historically used in Turkish carpets, as well as the weavings of the Hopi and the Navajo. Depending on the cultural tradition and the desired color, dyers use everything from the inner bark, roots, and twigs of the sumac.

In India, Pakistan, Nepal, Thailand, and southern China, the tannins in the heartwood of the cutch tree (*Acacia catechu*) dye browns from cinnamons to dark chocolates. Cutch is also often mixed with the nuts of the betel palm (*Areca catechu*) to make betel chew—a tooth-staining stimulant used by around 600 million people worldwide.

Lastly, dyers use tannins to create dark grays and blacks. Natural black dyes are hard to make, so they've been expensive and esteemed throughout history. One way to dye black is to create a reaction using tannins and iron (ferrous sulfate). Iron reacts with tannins to deepen pale, insipid colors to stone grays and black (a process explored in depth in Logwood, page 66). This combination of tannins and iron is an old method for making ink, too. First, oak galls are crushed and steeped in water until the liquid turns a murky, sepia brown. Then a small amount of ferrous sulfate is added, and the mixture instantly darkens to black. Most recipes then call for gum arabic, a natural resin made from hardened acacia tree sap that improves the ink's flow.

Iron gall ink goes back at least as far as the Romans: Pliny the Elder shared his recipe in 77 CE. Scribes penned the *Codex Sinaiticus*, the oldest known copy of the New Testament, in oak gall ink around 1,600 years ago. It subsequently became the most commonly used black ink for drawing and writing in Europe from the fifth century until the 19th century. The Magna Carta, Shakespeare's will, and Jane Austen's manuscripts were penned with oak gall ink, but it was also an ordinary ink used widely for letters and lists. Recipes vary a little—Austen, for example, added "strong stale beer" and a little sugar, while the British Government's official ink contained indigo, an addition that gave it a blue-black sheen.

But oak gall ink has a drawback: it can degrade over time. If the initial mix contains too much iron, the excess of iron sulfate slowly converts to sulfuric acid, causing everything from discoloration to brittleness to cracks and holes. Today, badly made ink continues to eat shadowy holes in old manuscripts, much to the chagrin of museum conservators everywhere.

An overdose of iron can damage fabrics, too. Sometimes, the fault isn't immediately apparent in freshly dyed fabrics (the exception to this is silk, which becomes instantly brittle). Instead, damage develops over months and years, creating craggy holes and stiffness in fabrics, so iron blacks have been routinely regulated and sometimes even banned. For instance, in 1480, members of the Venetian Arte Maggiore (a guild of wool dyers) were prohibited from keeping tannins and iron mordants in their workshops, as making cut-corner iron blacks risked their prestigious reputation. At other times and by other guilds, blacks made with iron were allowed but only if strict rules were followed. For example, dyers could use the tannins and galls as an overdye for woad, as going from blue fabric to black requires less iron (and a lower risk of damage) than starting with white or cream.

↓ Black walnut (*Juglans nigra*) in a forest of the Mississippi Valley, with American ornithologist Robert Ridgway seated at the base of the tree, 1881

The *Invisible* Ingredient

ONCE TANNINS AND MORDANTS have been applied as needed, you're finally ready to dye; a process that usually involves plonking your fiber or fabric into the dye pot and then patiently waiting. You'd think the careful steps taken up until this point would guarantee you good results, but you'd be wrong.

The final colors produced by natural dyes depend on the soil and water they're exposed to while growing, how and when they're harvested and processed, and even the weather outside on the day you dye. The particulars vary from dye to dye, but the one consistency is inconsistency—whether you're dyeing a single item in a kitchen pot, or a mass amount of cloth in a sprawling factory. Even something as basic as the water you're working with can impact the final color.

Water is perhaps the most crucial ingredient in the dyeing process, though it's generally overlooked, at least by novice dyers. But dyes need to be dissolved in a medium for them to work, and most often that medium is water; the innocuous liquid is also necessary for scouring, mordanting, using tannins, rinsing the finished textiles, growing natural dye plants, and processing synthetic dyes. But while it's glossed over at a craft scale, water is hard to ignore at an industrial one; brightly colored run-off from dye factories (and the blue dogs that stumble out of it) are perhaps the most visible aspect of the textile industry's pollution.

Getting the water right for a dye bath requires careful attention. Both hard water, which contains a high proportion of dissolved minerals like calcium and magnesium, and soft water, which doesn't, can inhibit the solubility of some dyes, meaning that the colors pulled from the dye pot will be muddier and less vibrant. For instance, cochineal (see page 108), will turn a muted purplish-pink in hard water, but in soft water the results are vivid and brilliant. Conversely, weld (see page 96) dyes pale, insipid yellows if soft water is used, but gives electric, sunshine yellows in hard water. Historic recipes often differentiate between using river water and rainwater versus water from a well for these reasons, as water that has sat underground often picks up minerals from its surroundings.

Traditionally, dyers would have been familiar with their local water supplies and skilled at adjusting recipes to compensate; for example, acids like vinegar or lemon juice counteract the mineral content in hard water. To this day, craft dyers will squeeze a lemon into their cochineal baths to coax out the brightest possible reds. Temperature plays a role, too. Use water that's too hot and some natural dyes will brown, changing from saturated yellows and reds to sallow hues the color of burnt toast.

On a commercial scale, the biggest issue with water and dyeing is just how much of it gets used, and how little of it is treated and cleaned before it's released into major water supplies and soils. Textile production is a thirsty industry, though statistics on water use are notoriously inaccurate. As water is used in so many aspects of textile production, from irrigating cotton to washing finished fabrics, and some of this can return relatively unsullied to the environment (if properly treated), just how much varies dramatically depending on how and where the cotton is grown, which dyes are used, and how the effluent is processed. Much of the water that can't be easily recovered is used in dyeing and finishing processes. And while developing new technological approaches is often considered the solution to adverse environmental consequences, at least one company has found early success by working with nature's seasonal cycles.

In the early 1980s, Vancouver-based printer Charllotte Kwon developed blood poisoning from her work running a Heidelberg press, which is a behemoth of a commercial letterpress machine. It took multiple blood transfusions to clear her system of the chemicals, heavy metals, and lead that had made their way into her blood from the inks and solvents used in the printing shop. After she recovered, Kwon quit the printing business and began searching for alternative ways to make colors that wouldn't poison the people who worked with them.

In 1986 she founded Maiwa, then a shop selling naturally dyed, artisan-produced goods, and now a textile school, foundation, producer, and retailer that works exclusively with natural dyes. In 1991 Kwon first traveled to India, home to some of the oldest natural dyeing traditions in the world, and has spent almost half her time there ever since. In the early 2000s, after a decade of research and exploration, she established a base on the outskirts of Jaipur, in the northern region of Rajasthan. Outside the city, residents have historically relied on wells for drinking water (some still do). The wells run deep into the desert soil; some are 50 feet deep, others 200—and in the past decades they've nearly all dried up.

In collaboration with local engineers and builders, Kwon is constructing a solar-powered dye factory in Bagru, a village about an hour's drive from Jaipur, that will use ancient construction techniques and trial a circular water system at a medium scale. Kwon estimates that they'll need 800,000 liters annually, an amount easily reached by the annual downpours from June through September. Channels will be cut into the soil to facilitate drainage into the water table, and wastewater will be filtered through a living system of plants, thrushes and mangroves, and reused.

Since they've begun developing the site, water has returned to the old well and is starting to trickle into the neighbors' properties too. According to Kwon, a river used to cut through the land, and she thinks it must still be there, somewhere. In time, she hopes it will return. An initiative like this offers hope. While it's currently far from a large-scale solution, Kwon's work shows that dyeing doesn't have to be a toxic enterprise.

↗ A view of riverside buildings from the Buriganga River, stained red from dye from tanneries which leak toxic waste

↓ Yarn dyeing at a vocational school for home economics in Brogård, Uppland, Sweden

Origins of Color —The Story So Far

Prehistory and the Ancient Mediterranean

It has been 26,000 years since humans began to dye. At least. Your great grandparents (999 times removed) were stirring a bubbling vat of dye long before the invention of modern agriculture, while woolly mammoths and sabertoothed cats roamed the earth. Our knowledge of these early color-seekers comes from microscopic fibers found in Dzudzuana, a cave in the Caucasus mountains in the west of the Republic of Georgia.

In 2007, Georgian archaeologist Eliso Kvavadze and her colleagues were excavating the cave when they came across over 1,000 fibers buried in clay samples from the site. These yarn fragments are the earliest samples of dyed textiles on record. They are black, gray, turquoise, and pink. They are also especially old and soft specimens—most of what's been unearthed by archaeologists is from the last 4,000 years and made of much harder stuff, because textiles tend to rot.

From the era of the Dzuduana fibers until about 2000 BCE the archaeological record of dyeing is scant: seeds from plants that were used for dyeing, the occasional fabric scrap, parts of looms, and a few papery-skinned mummies whose colorful burial clothing and shrouds have remained intact.

After 2000 BCE the evidence grows. More textiles survive from after this time and there are written records, too. Most of our knowledge from this era comes from a handful of Egyptian and Greco-Roman texts: the writings of the naturalist Pliny the Elder, the physician Dioscorides, the botanist Theophrastus, and the architect Vitruvius, and a pair of third-century papyri, documents written on a thick, plant-based, paper-like material. The papyri are named after Leyden (Leiden) and Stockholm, the cities where they sat untranslated for decades after being excavated from an Egyptian tomb in the early 1800s. The faded, fawn-colored Leyden Papyrus X comprises ten generously sized sheets folded lengthwise, with 111 recipes scrawled in black ink. There are instructions for making purple dye alongside advice for turning lead into gold, and pebbles into precious gems. The Stockholm papyrus is a similar document thought to be written by the same author. To supplement these texts there are numerous court records, laws, records of textile trade, and travelers' journals. It's also possible to glean insights from literature like Homer's epic poem *The*

↓ Skeins of wool dyed naturally with the root dye madder (*Rubia tinctorum*) drying outside a traditional carpet dyers workshop in Konya, Central Anatolia, Turkey, *c.*1960s

Iliad (c.700 BCE), where nestled among stories of mythical adventure there are references to dyes and the dyeing process.

If you've thought of people in the past dressed in pale beiges, faded grays, and dull browns you're only half right. While a relatively somber color palette was common for some clothing, like the workwear of laborers (which was often undyed), this wasn't the case across the board. Natural dyes provide a surprisingly brilliant array—you can get a host of lemon and golden yellows without much more than a potful of local weeds.

In the earliest days of textiles, cloth was spun, woven, and dyed at home with materials that would have been readily available. Thanks to the meticulous record keeping of an ancient Babylonian dye association, we know that by the second millennium BCE dyeing had become a profession. Aspiring dyers in Babylon (present-day Iraq) had to complete a rigorous five-year apprenticeship before their membership was approved.

At the time, professionally dyed cloth would have been expensive. Dyeing was a lengthy process, and to get even, saturated colors was no easy feat. It often required skilled labor and pricey imported ingredients. As a result, certain colors—like crimson reds and rich purples—tended to be worn only by the uber-rich. Aside from society's upper crust, people, especially in rural areas, continued to make and dye their own fabric.

Over the following centuries, cities like Tyre in Phoenicia (now Lebanon) grew into industrial centers famous for their dye workshops—and for the pungent smells that typified them. First-century Greek geographer Strabo deftly expressed the mixed blessing of Tyre's infamous stink: "The great number of dyeworks makes the city unpleasant to live in, yet it makes the city rich through the superior skill of its inhabitants."

By Strabo's era, dyeing had become big business. In Pompeii, an Italian city buried in ash and pumice by the eruption of Mount Vesuvius in 79 CE, archaeologists have uncovered several dye shops; some pots still contained purple dyes and the insects used to make red dye. The Roman god Mercury was carved above one such dye shop, holding a bag of money with the words *salve, lucrum* (welcome, profit) above him.

Ruling states often attempted to control the dye industry because of its value. Under the Roman emperor Alexander Severus (222–235 CE), the production of murex purple (see page 136), the most valuable color at the time, became a monopoly of the state. The fisherman, or *muriléguli*, were obligated to join a heavily regulated corporation and deliver quotas of the spiny, whorled mollusks to state-sanctioned dye houses. During the Byzantine Empire the same shellfish purple production reached its apex under the emperor Justinian (483–485 CE). According to the historian Procopius, Justinian handed the entire silk market over to an imperial treasurer, who skimmed himself off a hefty dividend, driving the silk workers, weavers, and dyers of Tyre and Beirut into poverty. Frustrated, many of the dispossessed workers migrated to Persia, where their skills were better compensated.

The dye industry continued to grow in power while the technical skills of the workforce developed in tandem. By the fall of the Western Roman Empire in the late fifth century CE, the Collegium Tinctorum, an ancient guild, distinguished six categories of artisans for the making of the color red alone. The most powerful among them were the *purpurarii*, who dyed the so-called royal purples, colors reserved for the emperor and his court. While the Eastern Roman Empire, or Byzantine Empire (which extended into what is now Turkey, Greece, Bulgaria, and parts of Italy), continued to be a powerful force for centuries, the Western Roman Empire collapsed and the Middle Ages descended on Europe, an era of technical stagnation that would last around a thousand years.

Medieval Europe (6th–15th Centuries)

During the Middle Ages, dyeing was dominated by organized professional associations called guilds that safeguarded members' common interests by offering protection and decent working conditions, and by eliminating competition. Nowhere were the guilds more influential than in the Medieval Italian city-states, which were semi-autonomous, powerful, and color-obsessed. In May of 1243, Venetian dyers created the oldest-known independent regulations for their profession. Brazilwood—a red dye from the heartwood of a tree that threatened the local insect-based scarlet industry—was banned.

The guild passed other strictures on apprenticeships, membership, and conduct, and the rules could be uncompromising. In 1255, statutes of a dyers' guild in Lucca, Tuscany, decreed any member who used an inauspicious red dyestuff would be fined 100 lire—enough to buy several small farms—or lose his right hand. While another guild, the Arte di Calimala in Florence, burnt any cloth not dyed to standard, and fined the dyers responsible. If the craftsman was unable to pay, off went one of their hands instead. While the guild system might have been behind a host of severed limbs, they had a reputation for looking out for their own.

The guild negotiated, provided for, and protected its members, while any dyer working outside this system seldom had access to the same standard of living.

Though the guilds were powerful, the social and financial status of professional dyers varied throughout the Medieval era in Europe. The fact that dyers often worked with materials like urine and blood meant that they were sometimes looked down upon even if they were financially successful. The 13th-century English grammarian John Garland suggested the only viable reason for a woman to marry a dyer was for his money, as the odors associated with the craft were enough to put off any other possible motivations. Still, capable dyers were often in demand. In the mid-14th century, the English king Edward III tried to woo Flemish dyers, from what is now Belgium, to England, and he wasn't alone in his courting; many cities offered incentives to foreign dye masters to set up trade within their walls.

As in ancient Rome, the status of dyers was often linked to the dyes that they worked with. Plain dyers were regularly separated from the so-called high dyers, who worked with more expensive materials and fabrics. In France, the lower echelon of color creators were known as *teinturiers en petit teint* (dyers of small dyes) and in Italy, *tintori d'arte minor* (dyers of the minor art). Plain dyers used comparatively simple recipes and inexpensive ingredients, though this was relative. Even an apprenticeship as a plain dyer lasted three years, followed by a further five years working as a journeyman in a licensed master's shop. After a total of eight years of training, dyers would go through a series of rigorous tests to earn the status of master.

Professionally dyed cloth was still expensive, and many people continued to make and dye it at home, especially in rural areas. The aforementioned Stockholm and Leyden papyri from the third century CE are forebears of a written tradition that was prevalent in pre-Enlightenment Europe, and which makes up most of what we know about domestic dyeing from this period. These tomes were dramatically titled "books of secrets."

Books of secrets are laced with esoteric wisdom, bringing together recipes, household remedies, and magical spells. The first, in a near-thousand-year tradition, was the *Kitāb al-Asrār*, or *Book of Secrets*, penned by the eminent Persian chemist and physician Abū Bakr Muhammad ibn Zakarīyā al-Rāzī (better known as Al-Rāzī) around 920 CE. Translations of this work circulated around Europe and were highly influential; the Latinized version of Al-Rāzī's name, "Rhazes" or "Rasis," pops up everywhere from Chaucer to medical textbooks.

Al-Rāzī's European successors copied his style and published their own books of secrets, which, with the invention of the printing press in the mid-15th century, were widely disseminated. The most famous of these works is the 1555 Venetian book, *I Secreti*, or *The Secrets of Alexis*, published under the pseudonym Alessio Piemontese. It was hugely popular, widely reprinted, and quickly translated into seven languages. The book includes a recipe for dyeing black that requires walnut juice and egg whites, a blue from elderberries, and "fair russet" made from brazilwood. An extensive section about stain removal and laundering accompanies more extraordinary folk remedies and medicines.

For instance, if you'd like to dream of wild beasts, the anonymous author recommends getting the heart of an ape and laying it under your head while you sleep. There's also an overnight recipe for healing hemorrhoids, cures for deafness, and holy water with many "notable virtues." The ingredients list of the latter would be at home on a modern menu alongside turmeric lattes and spirulina smoothies: cloves, nutmeg, ginger, pepper, sage, rosemary, marjoram, cinnamon, aloe, figs, raisins, dates, almonds, the kernels of a pineapple, and the petals of roses, both red and white.

The first dedicated Medieval dye manual, *The Plictho of Gioanventura Rosetti* (with the hefty subtitle *Instructions in the Art of the Dyers Which Teaches the Dyeing of Woolen Cloths, Linens, and Silk by the Great Art as Well as by the Common*) was published in Venice in 1548, marking a shift in who had access to information about dyeing. Previously this wisdom had been the domain of professional dye guilds and alchemists who jealously guarded their trade secrets. While books of secrets made dye recipes and techniques available to greater numbers of people, *The Plictho* offered a comparative wealth of technical information. The publication of *The Plictho* meant that aspiring dyers could avoid trawling through sections on wart removal and metallurgy to find a recipe for making red.

The Industrial Revolution and the Rise of the Scientific Method

The modern textile industry started to take shape from the 16th century onwards, thanks to the proliferation of written sources, the dissemination of Enlightenment ideas, and a boom in technological innovation. This era is comparatively well documented; there are a number of industrial and domestic dye manuals, as well as surviving notebooks and ledgers from dye companies that contain preserved fabric swatches and notes about customers' tastes, like "Mrs. Best thought these wines were too blue." There are patents on record for new equipment

↖ Color mixing of dyestuffs at the Print Works Division in Eddystone, Pennsylvania, *c.*1930s

↓ A plant dyeing course led by Helena Öberg, from Dvärsätt, Jämtland County in Hudiksvall, Sweden, *c.*1910

and dyes, trade documents, and company sales materials, and plenty of textiles and clothing have survived, too.

These artifacts all tell the same story: more textiles and dyes were being produced at lower prices than ever before. This proliferation of cloth happened for a few reasons. First, the production volume of textiles increased at great speed thanks to mechanization and improvements in agricultural techniques. By the late 18th century, inventions like James Hargreaves' spinning jenny, a machine that could spin fiber eight times faster than traditional spinning wheels, and Eli Whitney's cotton gin, which separated the hairy seeds from useable cotton fiber (previously a painstakingly slow job done by hand), were revolutionizing industries, and prices dropped accordingly. In Britain, for example, the cost of cotton cloth fell nearly one-third between 1770 and 1801, and dropped nearly half again by 1815. The situation was unprecedented—never had textiles been so cheap or so widely available.

Dye production increased in parallel, in part because most dyes at the time were derived from plants, and improved agricultural techniques, like better systems of crop rotation, soil drainage, and mechanized plows, meant that harvests were becoming more reliable. But there were other, far more sinister reasons for production increases and price drops, namely the rise of colonialism and slavery. A workforce made up of indentured and enslaved people in Europe's colonies (and later the independent nations in North and South America) provided the skilled labor that helped the dye and textile industries to expand.

It was during this time that the import of high-value dyestuffs from the colonies into Europe reached an industrial scale. Critical imports included cochineal (see page 108), a South American scale insect that is the source of a scarlet dye that became a Spanish monopoly, and indigo (see page 46), a blue dye that British colonial powers controlled the production of in India. These imports created price wars with locally produced dyes and spurred protectionist trade policies (see Woad, page 58, and Logwood, page 66).

The burgeoning field of chemistry also had an outsized effect on the dye industry. Chemistry had impacts on agriculture, like creating better fertilizers, which led to improved dye crop yields, but science had also begun to change the dyes themselves. For example, in the early 19th century, two French chemists found a way to purify alizarin, the main red colorant in madder, (a natural dye that comes from the roots of a shrub, see page 74), creating a supercharged dye that they called garancine (more on this in Alizarin, page 206).

As well as more concentrated versions of natural dyes, chemists endeavored to make new ones altogether. In 1771, British chemist Peter Woulfe was experimenting with the effects of nitric acid and indigo when he produced a buttery yellow crystalline solid. Woulfe had made the first synthetic dye, which was later named picric acid (from the Greek *pikros*, "bitter," for its acrid taste—it remains a mystery who in the lab performed the taste test). But picric acid never caught on as a dye; it didn't work well on cotton and it wasn't very lightfast—it was also highly flammable and frequently caught fire, a quality that led to its true success—as an ingredient in matches, explosives, and batteries.

The second synthetic dye was murexide, named after the murex group of mollusks that produce a purple dye that was at times more valuable than gold in Ancient Rome (see page 138). Murexide is a grape-purple color, and was made from uric acid, a chemical usually extracted from guano (the solidified droppings of birds, bats and seals). But murexide was only a modest success, and though neither it nor picric acid were commercial hits, these dyes set the stage for the tidal wave of change about to come.

The Shift to Synthetic (1856 to Mid-20th Century)

By the mid-19th century, dyeing was a large-scale industrial enterprise and chemists were playing an increasingly important role. Though the natural dye industry had scaled up and industrialized, it was about to be unseated by a cascade of cheaper, more reliable synthetic dyes in a seismic shift, kicked off by an accidental discovery made by 18-year-old English chemistry student William Henry Perkin, whose homegrown lab would produce the first commercially salient dye, mauveine (see page 188).

The vivid purple made Perkin a wealthy man at the age of 20, and over the next few years, a dozen new coal-tar colors came to market as others across Europe attempted to copy his success (see *Fossil Fuels*, page 185). As more synthetic colors hit the market, the natural dye industry began to falter.

Over the following decades, Germany became the center of the synthetic dye industry. Universities in Marburg, Göttingen, Heidelberg, Giessen, Berlin, Munich, Dorpat, and Keil had trained scores of ambitious young chemists, providing dye companies with an eager and well-trained talent pool. Germany's geography and geology poised them for further success. Although dyes were lightweight commodities that were easy to transport, even small-scale production required enormous amounts of fresh water, acids, alkalis, fuels, pyrites, salts, and coal tar, so new firms established operations along the Rhine River to facilitate production and transportation. The surrounding coal-rich Ruhr valley supplied the natural resources required to make dyes. In time, German dye manufacturers diversified, morphing into pharmaceutical giants that are still around today—companies like Bayer, which is famous for developing aspirin, and BASF, which invented both synthetic indigo and polystyrene. Profit from dye production meant these companies could invest in research and development, and the industry grew to include medicines, synthetic resins, explosives, and countless other materials.

By the 20th century, the German dye industry was seemingly unstoppable, and companies like BASF were strategic assets during the First World War. Germany's subsequent loss had lasting repercussions on the industry; trade blockades caused a necessary vogue for monochrome color palettes and then spurred new American dye competitors. Economic hardship pushed the German dye makers together, and in 1925, Bayer, BASF, and four others joined to create the chemical magnate IG Farben (roughly translated as the Syndicate of Dyestuff Industry Corporation). The consolidated chemical companies became infamous under the Nazi regime. Alongside making dyes, IG Farben ran a chemical factory at Auschwitz and manufactured Zyklon B, the lethal chemical released in gas chambers, among other atrocities.

After the Second World War, IG Farben was broken up and sold for parts, and the German dye industry was supplanted by its American competitors. Most well known is DuPont, a one-time gunpowder manufacturer in Delaware, which is responsible for synthetic consumer products including nylon, spandex, Kevlar, Teflon, and, of course, dyes.

In the second half of the 20th century, the production of dyes and chemicals shifted to countries with developing industrial sectors, including China, Bangladesh, and India. Ducol Organics, whose indigo waste dyed the dogs in Mumbai blue, is a subsidiary of Bayer, one of the original German dye makers.

FLORA

Indigo
Woad
Logwood
Madder
Safflower
Weld

Plants provided the most abundant and widely used dyes until just 170 years ago. Together, the dyes in this section created almost all the colored textiles in human history. Chosen for their popularity and notoriety, these dyes have dramatic social and economic histories.

The first dye featured is *Indigo*, the only plant-based blue in the world, made from the leaves of several dozen species found around the globe. Indigo is followed by *Woad*, Europe's primary source of indigo, and a singular plant with a big story. Next is *Logwood*, a source of black that was at the center of a decades-long trade war—its story is rife with pirates, blackmail, and thievery. In *Madder* you'll read about the oldest and most widely used red dye, followed by *Safflower*, a rare example of a plant that provides both yellow and red, used to color everything from the shrouds of Egyptian mummies to the cheeks of Japanese Geishas.

Finally, there is *Weld*, a weedy flower and the unlikely source of the brightest, best, and most popular yellow dye in the world.

Indigo

Indigofera tinctoria

Kingdom. Plantae

Order. Fabales

Family. Fabaceae

Other names. True indigo, Indian indigo, common indigo

Primary colorants. Indigotin, indirubin

Colors. Blues

Fastness. Excellent

Type of dye. Direct/vat

Other indigo-producing plants.

Indigofera arrecta. Bengal indigo, Java indigo

Indigofera suffruticosa. Bengal indigo, Natal indigo

Persicaria tinctoria (Polygonum tinctorium). Japanese indigo, Japanese knotweed

Wrightia tinctoria. Pala indigo, dyer's oleander

Isatis tinctoria. Woad—see page 58

INDIGO IS THE ONLY BOTANICAL, or plant-based, blue dye on earth and creates colors that range from pale, misty blue to inky midnight. Its source is counterintuitive: the small, green leaves of a few dozen plant species produce the world's best-loved blue dye. When processed, the leaves of indigo-producing plants become dense, navy bricks or dusty powders that can transform cloth from bland beiges into every shade of ocean and sky. The term *indigo* can refer to the dye, the plants that produce it, and a color: indigo is the inky hue sandwiched between blue and violet on the visible spectrum, allegedly placed there by Isaac Newton when he named the rainbow because of the ubiquity of the dyestuff.

Today, indigo is most recognizable for dyeing the world's most popular style of pants. In the 17th century an indigo-dyed cloth from Genoa, Italy, called Gene fustian twisted its way into the English language as *jeans*, as did *denim*, from *bleu de Nimes*, for a sturdy twill fabric woven in the French city of Nîmes. Levi Strauss's signature 501s, Daisy Duke's denim shorts, and the infamous "Canadian tuxedo" (a joking reference to a denim jacket and jeans combo) get their signature color from indigo.

The phrase *blue collar* owes its origin to indigo as well. The dye was so common in early 20th-century American workwear that it became shorthand for manual laborers, who wore dark, indigo-dyed clothes to hide the dirt of their daily toil. Indigo is the blue of Breton stripe tops, as recognizably French as baguettes and berets, and across the Atlantic was used to create Old Glory Blue, the official navy hue of the American flag. You'd be hard pressed to find a person in the industrialized world today who hasn't worn indigo-dyed clothing at some point in their lives.

Indigo's legacy of cultural and economic importance dates back millennia and is spread across the globe. The oldest known samples were excavated between 2007 and 2008 when archaeologists at Huaca Prieta, an ancient ceremonial site on Peru's north coast, found sooty cotton fabric scraps sandwiched, cement-like, in the layers of a temple's foundation. They had been buried for six millennia and were a drab, muddy brown thanks to the rubble and ash that had kept them out of the sunlight.

Jeffrey Splitstoser was the archaeologist and textile expert charged with cleaning the fabric. As he carefully washed the fibers he was surprised at how drastically they changed. Soft blue yarns started to appear, woven between cream and white ones. Using high-performance liquid chromatography (HPLC) and photodiode-array detection (HPLC-PDA), Splitstoser and his team coaxed out the blue dyes' chemical makeup. Unknowingly, they had found the world's earliest known samples of indigo.

While the Peruvian fabrics from Huaca Prieta are the oldest samples known, indigo gets name-dropped everywhere—from ancient Sanskrit poems to Javanese charts. It turns up in the classical Graeco-Roman empire: in the first-century CE writings of the Roman architect Vitruvius and the Roman naturalist Pliny the Elder, and in the works of the Greek physician and author Dioscorides, from the same era. The word "indigo" is from the Greek *indikon*, meaning "a substance from India," where it has a long history of cultivation and trade.

There is no one reason for indigo's longevity and popularity, though it could have something to do with the near-magical transformation of green leaf to blue dye. Moreover, indigo is very light- and wash-fast, which means that it doesn't fade when exposed to sunlight and laundering. When indigo does fade, it's usually because of rubbing (also called crocking), which is how dark denim jeans get their characteristic hip creases, pale knees, and smartphone silhouettes on back pockets after a few months of wear. Unlike other dyes that fade to browns and yellows, indigo blues pale into softer versions of themselves as time passes. And while there are a few red dyes and dozens of yellow ones, through most of human history indigo has been the only blue.

Indigo is a singular dye, but it comes from a host of plant species: *Indigofera tinctoria*, or true indigo, is the most common plant source of the dye today. It's a bushy shrub in the bean family with delicate oval leaves and blush-pink flowers. The light, sky blue fabric scraps found at Huaca Prieta could be from an *Indigofera*, or *Justicia colorifera* (*Cuaja tinta* or *Tinta montes*). *Indigofera suffruticosa* is Guatemalan or wild indigo, and *I. arrecta* is Bengal or Java indigo (though it is native to Africa). Japanese indigo is *Persicaria tinctoria* or *Polygonum tinctorium*, and woad, aka *Isatis tinctoria*, is the primary indigo-supplying plant in Europe—more on that later.

↖ Blue printing at the H. Fischer dye works, eastern Germany, 1940

↓ A group of workers beating oxygen into indigo vats with wooden paddles as their supervisors watch. These factories often relied on indentured labor and other abusive working conditions. Allahabad, India, 1877

There are dozens of indigo-producing plants, and while all of them make the same blue dye, they don't contain the same concentration of the color. In general, *Indigofera* species are the most potent sources—they flourish in warm, humid, and sunny climates, and, consequently, countries in the southern hemisphere and around the equator have some of the richest indigo traditions. Species that grow in cooler regions, like woad, usually have lower concentrations of dye, which means it takes more of them to match the deep blues of their warm-weather counterparts. So when trade in tropical indigo spread more readily through the moderate climates of Europe in the 17th century, the woad industry (a powerful commercial player) tried everything from slander campaigns to protectionist trade policy to defend its share of the market. Later, as the colonizing forces of Western Europe moved into territories with indigo-suitable climates, they tried to get in on the blue-dye action themselves, starting new production initiatives or taking brutal control of existing ones.

That cultures around the world have figured out how to make indigo dye is impressive, since making blue liquid from small green leaves is not a straightforward process. While you can throw other dyestuffs like madder roots, oak bark, or a weld plant into a simmering pot of water for an hour and get a dye, to do the same with an indigo plant will leave you no better off than when you started. This is because there is no actual indigo in indigo-producing plants. While most plants contain the chemical compounds, or colorants, that work as dye—madder contains alizarin and purpurin, oak bark has tannins, and weld has flavonoids—indigo does not.

Instead, indigo plants contain precursors. These precursors are indigo's forerunners: chemicals that have the potential to become blue dye. In tropical indigo plants, this precursor is indican, in woad, isatan B. To turn them into indigo, these precursors first need to hydrolyze, or react with water, to form indoxyl. Then, indoxyl reacts with oxygen and transforms into indigotin, the dark blue compound responsible for indigo dye. Though they are used somewhat interchangeably, the term *indigotin* is more precise than indigo, which can refer to the plants, the dyes, or the color. Small amounts of other colorants are at work in the indigo vat, too, like *indirubin*, or indigo-red, which adds purplish depth to the dye—so distinguishing between indigo and indigotin is helpful for clarity.

But there's yet another step in the process—indigotin isn't soluble. It's part of a group of dyes called vat dyes which won't dissolve in water alone. To make a useful dye out of indigotin it must be reduced, meaning that the oxygen must be removed. Reducing indigotin turns it into leuco-indigo, or indigo white, a shimmering, pale yellowish substance that is soluble. Once you've got a bath of reduced indigo—called a vat—you're ready to dye, though even as you pull the cloth out of an indigo bath it won't be blue. Instead, it will be a radioactive fluorescent green, and for a moment the transformation will seem impossible. But then the cloth hits the air, leuco-indigo reacts with oxygen, and transforms into indigotin, now stuck tight to the fiber, and the color turns from acid green to cornflower blue. To go from light blues to dark, pieces of cloth are repeatedly dipped in the vat—as many as 100 times.

In practice, dyers use different techniques to get this chemical reaction and unlock denim-dark hues from jade-green indigo leaves. The method historically used at commercial scale turns indigo into dense cakes that are compact, light, easy to transport and will stay potent for centuries. Recently, one adventurous English dyer achieved beautiful blues with indigo found on the wrecked remains of the *Svecia*, a Swedish East India Company ship that sank off the coast of Scotland in 1740.

Over the years these little indigo cakes have been mistaken by Europeans for powdery rocks, though the record was set right in the 13th century by Marco Polo's travelogue. Famously, the young Venetian merchant traveled East with his family and spent decades in Asia before returning to Venice. His account of the journey is part autobiography, part travel guide, and part fairy tale (think weather-controlling wizards and unicorns the size of elephants). In *The Travels of Marco Polo* he details the cultivation of indigo with a fair amount of accuracy; however, misinformation about the source of the dye persisted for centuries. As late as 1705, permission was granted to build a mine in Germany, with indigo listed as a mineral to extract from the earth.

Given that indigo is an ancient dye that requires such a complex process, it's not surprising that it has been the source of superstition. For instance, if there is a death in the village, the Toba Batak of northern Sumatra rush to put lids on their pots to protect the dye's spirit from invasion by the dead, safeguarding its ability to produce color. Dyers in Thailand practice a similar ritual. In India, Tamil women call their laments *nilappaddu*—blue or dark songs. The mourners themselves are *nilamma*, blue women. Among the Omani Bedoin, indigo's nickname is *haras*, "the guardian," and underclothing is dyed blue to win or regain the favor of the Zar, evil pre-Islamic spirits.

In certain contexts, indigo is considered a powerful protector or a status symbol, and is even connected to fertility and life cycles. It attracts a certain romanticism, but it also has a much darker history. Dye manufacturing industrialized in the 18th and 19th centuries as European colonial domination spread across the world, and indigo, like sugar, tea, and rum, became one of the great colonial commodities. The British East India Company set its sights on Bengal, a north Indian region with a long history of indigo dyeing. In time, the area became the world's leading supplier.

Companies implemented industrial versions of traditional production methods, which stank and produced toxic fumes so vile that the French encyclopedist Diderot named them *le diablotin*—the devil's tanks. Workers spent hours pacing up and down the swimming pool-sized tanks with wooden paddles, or, worse, bare hands, to beat oxygen into the slimy mix of rotting indigo leaves, water, and lime. Prolonged exposure could lead to headaches, impotence, and cancer. Even at the time, workers were aware of the risk, and the few safety measures that were in place are less than convincing. One treatise from 1705 recommends drinking milk every half hour to stave off indigo's ills.

Conditions for Bengal indigo growers were hardly better. For decades, the peasant farmers, or ryots, worked on leased land in a system of indentured labor. They were kept in debt, prevented from growing subsistence crops like rice, and regularly whipped and beaten. In 1859 the ryots rebelled, some choosing peaceful resistance, and others burning down indigo depots where the dye was stored and executing the British indigo growers. Afterwards, a shaken British government created the "Indigo Commission" and conducted an extensive inquiry. Even its own agents admitted the working conditions were abysmal. They found that hundreds of contracts made between ryots and the planters were forgeries (in one case the ryot in question had died several years before the agreement was written). Likewise, an 1861 article in the *Calcutta Review* claimed: "not a chest of Indigo reached England without being stained with human blood." In the same year, the satirical play *Nil Darpan*, or *The Indigo Planting Mirror*, received extensive press coverage for its critical depiction of the English as brutal overlords, making explicit the struggle of the indentured Indian peasantry.

India wasn't alone in the violence of its indigo industry; coercion of labor forces was common around the globe. Records from the West Indies and American colonies detail the use of indigo as a currency to purchase enslaved people. Until recently, however, most histories of indigo have championed the landowners, slave owners, and others in power. For example, a White woman named Eliza Pinckney is credited with jumpstarting the South Carolina indigo industry in the 1740s, but recent reports have brought to light the contributions of John "Quash" Williams, an enslaved Black man who may have been the architect of Pinckney's success.

In South America, Guatemala became a center of indigo production under Spanish colonial rule in the 1700s. Plants used to make indigo dye were exported from El Salvador, Nicaragua, Honduras, Mexico, Ecuador, and Peru, and during the peak of the South American indigo trade in the 18th century more than a million pounds of the dyestuff were exported to Spain.

But the age of indigo was not to last. In 1897, chemists created a commercially viable synthetic indigo. It was the last of the key natural dyes to be synthesized, and this new invention would decimate the natural indigo industry in less than a decade (a story that unfolds in *Fossil Fuels*, see page 185).

Still as popular today as it ever was, indigo was the first dye to be considered for a widescale natural revival. Stony Creek Colors, an ex-tobacco farm in Tennessee, founded the first commercial natural indigo factory in the United States in over a century. From Tamil Nadu to Bengal, Indian production of natural indigo is making a comeback. Some of this new generation of indigo producers are descendants of those once forced to make the blue dye for the British, opening a new chapter in their country's long history of indigo. In Japan, Buaisou, a company farming and dyeing with indigo, rekindled *sukumo*, a traditional fermentation technique for making the dye that it grows and processes—even collaborating with beauty giants Aesop and The Body Shop, and with shoe companies like New Balance and Nike.

Although natural indigo production is on the rise, it is not likely to outperform its synthetic cousin. According to one estimation, replacing the current global production of synthetic indigo with natural dyes would amount to around 80 times more in production costs. So unless the world suddenly loses interest in indigo after millennia, the natural version of this beloved color is likely to remain a comparatively small-scale affair.

→ Two Japanese women wearing conical sugegasa straw hats treat indigo plants to be used for aizome dyeing, 1919

A Recipe for *Saxon* Green

This recipe is adapted from Ellis Asa's *The Country Dyer's Assistant* (1798), one of the first American dye treaties. Asa has a lot to say about indigo: the best quality comes from the Spanish colonies (modern Jamaica, Haiti, and Guatemala) and is fine, soft, and floats on the surface of water, but this top-tier indigo was so expensive that it was rarely used as a dye on its own by domestic dyers. Instead, it was stretched out with fustic, a yellow dye from the heartwood of a tree in the mulberry family, to make Saxon green, a leafy hue popular at the time.

To make Saxon green, take three ounces of good indigo and pound it until you can run it through a fine sieve. Add your prepared indigo to a small vessel and gradually add a pound of oil of vitriol (an archaic term for sulfuric acid), stirring for one hour. Let the mixture stand for a day, stirring occasionally. After standing, the indigo mix will be ready for use. In this state the mixture can be stored in a glass bottle fitted with a stopper of beeswax and kept for up to a year.

To dye 20 yards of fulled cloth (generally a thick wool fabric), 25 yards of baize (a midweight wool fabric), or 30 yards of thin cloth, put 10 pounds of good fustic that has been cut into chips into a copper (a cauldron-like pot) filled with clean water. Bring the water almost to a boil. Keep at this heat for eight or nine hours. Let the bath cool and take out the chips, laying them out to dry, as they can be "profitably employed" in dyeing common drab.

Heat the fustic dye again and dip your cloth for half an hour. Remove the cloth and allow the bath to cool. Add four pounds of alum to the dye, skimming the filth that will rise to the top. Dip the cloth again for an hour in the cooled water, then remove. Bring the dye to a boil and add seven or eight spoonfuls of your indigo mix. Let the mixture boil for a few minutes, stir it well, then dip the cloth for half an hour, turning it briskly. Now remove the cloth from the dye bath and let it cool. Repeat the dipping and cooling in this manner until the color is obtained. Rinse and dry the cloth.

Woad

Isatis tinctoria

Kingdom. Plantae

Order. Brassicales

Family. Brassicaceae

Other names. Pastel, guede, guado, glasto, vitrum, glastum

Primary colorants. Indigotin, indirubin

Colors. Blues

Fastness. Excellent

Type of dye. Direct/vat

AS A BOY, THE IRISH SAINT CIARÁN of Clonmacnoise was more mischievous than his holy status might suggest. The 15th-century *Book of Lismore*, a Gaelic manuscript that contains the great stories of medieval Irish literature, sets out the tale:

One day, Ciarán's mother was preparing to dye some cloth blue with woad, a spindly flowering plant in the mustard family and source of indigo (for more on indigo, see the previous entry). Though it's less potent than most tropical indigo producers, woad was the biggest source of blue dye in medieval Europe, and creates the same palette, ranging from powder blue to navy.

In Irish folklore it's bad luck to have men and boys around the dye pot, so Ciaran's mother ordered her son out of the family home as she prepared her woad vat. Ciarán, sullen and spiteful at being sent away, cursed the dye as he went out the door. When his mother pulled her cloth from the vat, she found dull gray stripes all over her newly blue fabric. She scolded Ciarán—who had snuck back in—believing him to be responsible for the dull transformation, and kicked him out of the house again, but this only drove him to curse the vat once more and the cloth was bleached white.

His mother pleaded with him to cease his cursing, and Ciarán relented. He blessed the dye vat, and it became the strongest dye they'd ever seen —even, as the legend goes, able to dye the local cats and dogs a shocking shade of ultramarine.

The history of woad is brimming with stories like the myth of Saint Ciarán. Some of these are superstitious tales and others have political and economic origins. In the region of Thuringia (now central Germany), scheming dyers who used madder red argued that hell must in fact be blue, and paid glass-makers to make the devils in their stained-glass windows cobalt, instead of the usual red. Farther north, in Magdeburg, madder dyers hired fresco painters to create cerulean hellscapes in a similar effort to tarnish woad's reputation.

Woad (*Isatis tinctoria*) was the primary source of blue dye in Europe for millennia. While it contains a different precursor—the chemical present in the leaves that have the potential to become blue dye—than other indigo-producing plants, the colorants at the end of the process are the same. This means it produces the same denim blues, though part of woad's popularity was that it could be used as a "top" and "bottom" dye—a base or overdye for many other colors. Combined with weld, one of the most widely used yellow dyes and the subject of a later chapter, woad could make Lincoln, Kendal, and Saxon greens. Mixing woad with madder, kermes, or orchil produced pinks, purples, scarlets, and even blacks. Among the many indigo producers, European woad has earned its own entry because of the size of its industry, its cultural salience, and the contentious trade relationship with the tropical indigo industry.

Woad is native to the Mediterranean and western Asia. There is currently no way of tracking its migration across Europe, but its use had spread to Britain by the Iron Age (*c.*1200–500 BCE). Slim stalks with small, yellow flowers grow from a central rosette, a collection of strap-like leaves at the base of the plant, pushing skyward.

Like other sources of indigo, making dye from woad is complex and labor-intensive. A traditional processing method goes as follows: After the first season of growth, woad leaves are ground into a paste. Then, they are shaped by hand into balls and left for weeks to dry (exactly how long depends on the weather). During this time, they shrink to a tenth of their original size and a quarter of their original weight. After the balls dry and harden, they are pulverized and couched—splattered with water and allowed to ferment. Once dried, woad contains pigment 20 times stronger than in the same quantity of fresh leaves. It's a foul-smelling process: woad production smelled so bad that Elizabeth I banned its manufacture within eight miles of her palaces. One contemporary dyer described the scent of woad to me as "rotten cabbagey."

But even after weeks the dried woad still won't work as a dye. Woad is a vat dye, which means it is insoluble and must be reduced, or chemically changed into a substance that will dissolve in water, in order to work. Dyers do this through another round of fermentation, creating the vat. Recipes call for mixing solutions of woad, water, and urine with ground madder roots or wheat bran. From this point, the woad can take up to a month to ferment enough to become a usable dye.

Woad is best known in the popular imagination as the blue warpaint attributed to the ancient Celts in Hollywood blockbusters like *Braveheart*.

↖ Woadmen balling the woad, Parson Drove, Cambridgeshire, England, *c.*early 20th century

↓ Woad stamp, pail, and seed sifter at Skirbeck Woad Mill, Lincolnshire, England, 1935

But the reality of these blue-painted people remains contested. Julius Caesar's often-cited *De Bello Gallico* describes people covered in *vitrum*, which was translated as woad in a 1565 version of the book; however, the word could also mean "glaze" or "glass." Although the Roman poet Marital also mentions the "woad-stained Britons" and Pliny the Elder, writing in 77 CE, notes that women in Britain used woad to stain their bodies during sacred rites.

While the verdict is still out on whether the Celts stained their bodies blue, woad paint appears regularly enough in historical accounts to warrant some speculation on the matter. Scholars and wannabe woad painters have debated whether or not it's possible—some claim the dye is caustic on skin and others that it produces a smudgy mess instead of a workable paint. But Simone Parrish, a self-described "bard, cook, neck-lace maker, woad painter, and logistics wrangler" in a Celtic living history group, has proven them wrong. She's been using woad for body painting for the last 20 years, proving that it is possible. Her recipe: 5 g powdered woad, 2 tsp whisky, and a pinch of rosemary (to combat what she describes as the mixture's "wet dog" smell).

The blue, fact or fiction, saturates Celtic history, and woad's popularity among the tribes of Northern Europe gained it an unsavory reputation in the Roman Empire. By the 11th century, blue was gaining some good press in the Mediterranean, when it began to be associated with the Virgin Mary. In portraits from this era the Mother of God is shrouded in blue cloth, evoking her mourning and her divinity. Once associated with warfare and savagery, blue was starting to be seen as softer, more gentle—and pious.

From the 13th to the 16th centuries, woad enjoyed a surge in popularity, earning it the nickname "blue gold" and creating unprecedented wealth where it was grown. In the South of France, the Languedoc region became a prosperous center for production. Dried woad was known as pastel (from "paste") or *guède*. Between 500 and 700 mills operated around Toulouse, and stately houses still pepper that landscape, remnants of a booming bygone age. In the 16th century, woad was the second biggest import to England from France, after wine. Its trade was such big business that unarmed ships received special permission to enter ports with woad even during times of war.

In Medieval Germany, like in France, the woad industry brought prosperity. The central German region of Thüringia was once the wealthy home of the *Waidstädt*, or woad towns: Erfurt, Gotha, Langensalza, Ternstedt, and Arnstadt. Now, disused mills sit at the centers of these towns, and old millstones still dot the countryside. Rich woad merchants earned the nickname *Waidherrn*: "gentleman of woad." But not everyone thought the plant a worthwhile crop. In 1531, Protestant Reformation leader Martin Luther complained in his book *Table Talk* that woad depleted soil quality. He claimed that peasants were using farmland for woad, "where good and noble grain used to be cultivated."

The Age of Pastel came to an end in the 17th century as Europeans began importing tropical indigo on a large scale. The woad industry struggled to keep pace, as this dyestuff has lower concentrations of indigo precursors than many tropical indigo plants, meaning you need a lot more of it and the dyes tend to be weaker. Moreover, indigo's high concentration of precursors means that it works well on cellulose fibers like cotton and linen that don't readily dye (see book 2: *The Dyeing Process* for more on this) as well as protein fibers such as wool and silk, while woad works only on protein. At the time, imported Indian cottons were surging in popularity, and indigo dyers jumped on the coattails of this market. Very quickly the more adaptable, imported indigo started to flood the market, and the domestic woad industry couldn't keep up.

At first, the industry tried to stave off the influx by banning local dyers from using Indian indigo. In Britain, Queen Elizabeth I banned its import, while in Germany several cities put local prohibitions in place, some of which would last over 100 years. Even at the end of the 18th century, magistrates in Nuremberg made dyers swear annual oaths that they weren't using indigo—under penalty of death. Before this, in 1609, Henri IV of France forbade the importation of indigo, also threatening the death penalty. Slander campaigns cropped up to discourage the use of imported indigo—pamphlets were distributed, bills set into motion, and the Holy Roman Emperor even issued imperial decrees. In Germany, it was dubbed "the devil's dye"; in Britain, "food for the devil." It's falsely described in dye manuals from the time as poisonous, corrosive, and unreliable.

But tropical indigo's ascension could not be stopped. It was cheaper and more potent than woad, and readily available from trade along the Silk Road to the east and Spanish colonies in the West Indies. Indigo production relied on indentured and slave labor, so the costs to make it were significantly lower than European woad pastel, even though it was brought to the continent across long distances. By the late 19th century the only woad production of any note that was maintained in Europe was in support of making indigo using imported dyes and plants. The dye vat would ferment more quickly if a little couched woad was added to the mix.

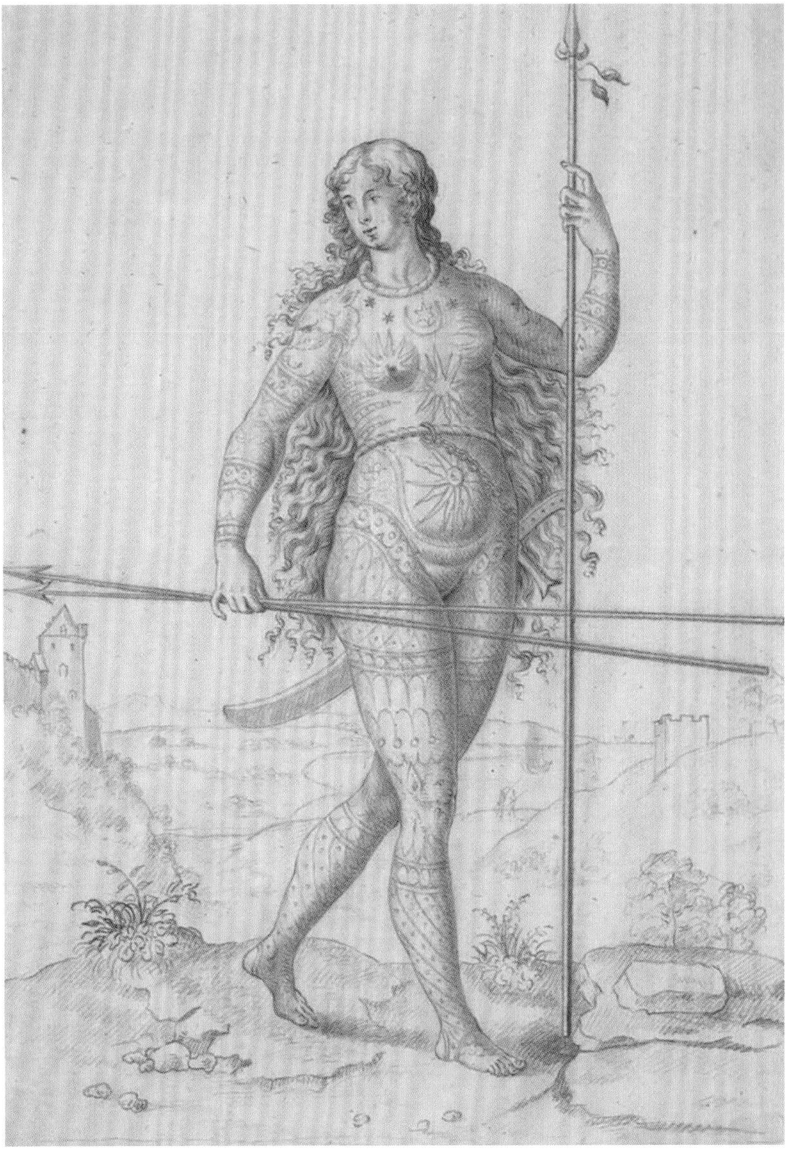

→ A married woman Pict, after a drawing by John White in Thomas Hariot, *A Briefe and True Report of the New Found Land of Virginia*, 1590

Logwood

Haematoxylum campechianum

Kingdom. Plantae

Order. Fabales

Family. Fabaceae

Other names. Campeachy wood, bloodwood tree, palo de campeche, palo de tinte, palo negro, spiny tree

Primary colorant. Hematoxylin

Colors. Blue-violets, grays, blacks

Fastness. Fair–good, increased by an iron mordant

Type of dye. Adjective/mordant

PHILLIP THE GOOD (1396–1467), Duke of Burgundy, was a 15th-century style icon who ushered in a continental trend for black. He was a young, powerful, and handsome monarch and though he started wearing black to mourn his father's death, it became a lifelong uniform.

At the time, wearing black was intended to indicate seriousness. Monks had begun wearing black robes a few decades earlier, making the shade a symbol of moral virtue and sobriety. At the same time, the European merchant class was growing in wealth and influence, threatening the status of the aristocracy. To try to keep the upstarts in their place (unsuccessfully, on most occasions), the monarchies established a series of sumptuary laws intended to restrict lavish personal spending. The laws banned luxurious scarlets and peacock blues for everyone except the upper crust. Paired with Phillip's fashion influence and black's moral overtones, these sumptuary laws helped kickstart a trend for the shade that swept Europe's merchant class and beyond.

Black is a notoriously tricky color to dye. Even with modern synthetics, it's a color prone to fading—as the washed-out grays of old T-shirts stand testament. Before synthetic dyes, dyers created black fabric in two ways: with iron mordants or by overdyeing. Overdyeing starts by dyeing fabric a dark color; in Europe, dyers usually used woad. Then the cloth is dyed again; with madder, walnut, alder, or chestnut. Woad dyeing on its own is a lot of work—adding an extra step and another dyestuff only upped the cost. The second method for making black relies on a chemical reaction between ferrous sulfate (iron) and tannins. Tannins are long molecules that make dark chocolate taste bitter and are responsible for coffee and red wine staining your teeth (they're also the subject of *Astringent Color* in this book's introduction).

Historically, the tannins for dyeing usually came from oak galls—small, round growths caused by gall wasps laying their eggs in oak trees. The wasp secretes a hormone, and the tree reacts with a tannin-rich growth that resembles a yellowish-brown ping pong ball. Most galls are smooth, but some are covered in tiny ridges. Once the eggs hatch, the wasps fly on, and the galls are left dangling from the trees, no longer needed by the wasps but useful for dyeing and a key ingredient in most early inks. The first recorded use of oak gall inks is in Pliny the Elder's first-century writings, but the process could be much older—it is unknown who first discovered that galls could be used to make stable brown-black inks and dyes. Oak bark is sometimes used in dyeing for its high tannin content, and an unsuspecting dyer could have included some galls on a whim and been thrilled at the result.

Dyeing with tannins and iron makes jet blacks, but they're not perfect. For one, using iron brings the risk of corroding the fibers. Over time, the ferrous sulfate in these dyes can convert into sulfuric acid, which weakens fibers. In old tapestries, areas dyed black sometimes look like they've been swarmed by moths, an appearance caused by this corrosion. In addition, the production of oak galls relies on the life cycle and fickle nesting choices of wasps, a species that is impossible to farm. There are also many kinds of gall, with differing amounts of tannin. Ultimately, making black this way can quickly become an expensive headache.

All this to say that when Spanish conquistadors landed in Mexico's Yucatan peninsula in 1519 and saw the locals in beautiful black clothing, they saw dollar signs, and greedily sought the source of the color. The dye they sought came from the heartwood, or the innermost core, of a spiny, gray-barked tree with delicate, heart-shaped leaves, called logwood.

Logwood's scientific name, *Haematoxylum campechianum*, hints at both its use and its source. *Haematoxylum* is from the Greek—*haima*, for blood, and *xylon*, wood, for the tree's crimson heartwood. *Campechianum* refers to the Bay of Campeche, where the Spanish first encountered the tree.

Logwood thrives in the watery landscape of mangroves and marshes along the coast of Mexico and South America. Its trunk is narrow and crooked, and it has clusters of frothy, yellow blossoms. The wood is both hard and heavy, and while the outer wood is pale, logwood's inner core is stained dark reddish-brown, hinting at its potential as a dye. Indigenous civilizations in the region used logwood for several millennia as a dye and as medicine before the Spanish conquistador Hernan Cortez and his cronies showed up. Aztecs and Mayans treated various ailments with logwood, including anemia, dysentery, diarrhea, tuberculosis, and menstrual cramps.

On its own, logwood dyes cloth a blueish purple, but it's a chameleon when combined with different mordants—the metal salts that form chemical bridges between dyes and fibers making dyes more permanent and sometimes changing the color palette. For example, when logwood is used with a zinc sulfate mordant it produces eggplant purples; when mixed with mercury chloride it produces oranges and reds like the colors of autumn leaves. Meanwhile, using a potassium arsenate mordant will shift logwood to a rich, golden amber dye. The natural colorant responsible for this rainbow potential is called hematoxylin, a clear crystal that gives the heartwood its reddish hue.

Alongside hematoxylin there are traces of other colorants including a derivative of brazilein—the colorant found in brazilwood, a tree that is the source of a bright red dye and the plant the nation of Brazil was named after. Five other colorants have yet to be isolated and named. Crucially, logwood contains large amounts of tannins, which play a vital role in its history as a black dye. Hematoxylin dyes cloth brilliant colors, but the dyes fade into paler, muddier versions when exposed to sunlight. An iron mordant will react with the tannins in logwood, making these fickle dyes darker and more permanent, which is why it's been so valued as a black.

Like other sources of black, logwood must be layered with various dyes or combined with iron. But it has a few advantages over its competitors. Dyeing with logwood is simpler and cheaper than overdyeing woad and indigo. The heartwood of the logwood tree is made into woodchips or ground into powder and then boiled in hot water to make the dye. Both indigo and woad require much more elaborate processing (see pages 46 and 58, respectively) and consequently are more expensive. Logwood makes deep, even blacks that are rich, lustrous, and seductive; they are as beautiful as the blacks made from overdyes, but cost a fraction of the price.

Logwood quickly gained popularity in Europe. At first Spain had a monopoly on the trade, and the limited supply meant logwood became so valuable that it was subject to rampant piracy—primarily by the English. During the reign of Henry VIII (1509–1547) one shipload of logwood was worth a year's trade in any other cargo. But like indigo, brazilwood, and other new imports, it was met with resistance. In 1581, Henry's daughter, Queen Elizabeth I, the queen of outlawing colors, banned logwood

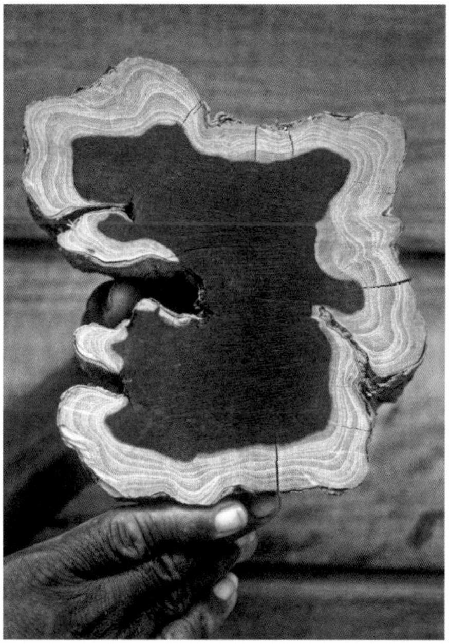

↗ Deep-blue rings of the logwood, or campeche, tree in Guadeloupe, French West Indies

↓ Logwood processing near Campeche, Mexico, 1884

importing and dyeing, blaming its poor lightfastness, but protectionist trade policy was the more likely motivation for the ban. England had a flourishing woad industry and logwood was a threat. Records show that some dyers ignored the law and imported logwood anyway.

Other countries contested Spain's claim to the Yucatan and its logwood. In 1494 the Portuguese and the Spanish signed the Treaty of Tordesillas, ostensibly splitting the Atlantic world (what was known of South America and the Caribbean) between the two countries. But they were not the only ones with claims to the land, least of all the people who already lived there. By 1519—when Cortez landed in the Yucatan—France, Holland, and England were among a host of European nations fighting for a slice of the "new world."

By 1585, a tense trade dispute between England and Spain erupted into a decades-long trade war, and logwood was one of the commodities at its center. Breaking Spain's monopoly on logwood was considered a key factor in the sinking of the Spanish Armada in 1588. Legally, the coastal regions where logwood grew belonged to the Spanish, so the English logwood cutters and the merchants that bought their wares were considered pirates. But that didn't stop the English from cutting logwood and raiding Spanish ships to steal it.

Early logwood cutters were a motley crew from a mix of backgrounds: ship captains, pirates, merchants, and men who had escaped slavery in the Caribbean. But they had one thing in common—they wanted quick cash, and were willing to trespass on Spanish land to get it. The logwood industry was illegal and dangerous, and it paid proportionately to the risks.

The early logwood camps set up in the marshy landscapes were basic and the work was brutal—think hard, physical labor in mosquito-filled swamps. Cutters felled the trees with hatchets and axes, chipping, carrying, and loading the wood into canoes. Thunderstorms and heavy rain characterize the hot, muggy wet season in the Yucatan, and even in the dry season enough rain would fall to form temporary creeks big enough to transport the logwood. The heavy rain and flood-prone landscape made setting up comfortable settlements challenging, to say the least, and the cutters had to build raised sleeping platforms to avoid getting soaked by midnight floods. There were unwanted visitors, too; the Spanish authorities ousted the logwood cutters from their camps several times. Since cutting was profitable, they kept returning, ignoring treaties and navigation acts. One cutter, "Daniel the Irishman," was attacked and nearly eaten by an alligator, but even that didn't stop him seeking his logwood fortune—he returned the next season with a limp.

Transporting logwood to Europe was risky, too. On the open seas, pirate attacks were expected and often overlooked by officials on all sides. Countries didn't have national navies as we know them today; instead, royal fleets would work on contract. A captain might hire his ship as a merchant vessel, then a naval vessel, with a bit of smuggling in between.

Though logwood continued to be imported into England the law against the practice didn't change until 1662. After that, the English founded an official colony in the Bay of Honduras, but the cutters who had been operating there illegally for decades were not interested in following official rules. Instead of shipping the logwood to London as expected, the rogue cutters would sell it to whoever paid the highest price, whether in Germany, Holland, or the American colonies.

As the logwood industry legitimized, more cutters moved into the area. Merchants and tradesmen followed and the settlement grew. In the 18th century, mahogany wood became another key commodity for the region, requiring more manpower than logwood and leading to an increased reliance on slave labor. Over time, the English settlements in the Bay of Honduras became the country of Belize. A pair of logwood cutters mark this troubled history on the nation's flag.

Madder

Rubia tinctorum

Kingdom. Plantae

Order. Gentianales

Family. Rubiaceae

Other name. Dyer's madder

Primary colorants. Alizarin, purpurin, pseudo-purpurin

Colors. Reds, from pale pinks to bricks

Fastness. Excellent

Type of dye. Mordant/adjective

Other sources of madder.

Rubia peregrina. Wild madder

Rubia cordifolia. Indian madder, munjeet

Rubia sikkimensis. Naga madder

Relbunium ciliatum. Antanco, chamiri, chapi chapi

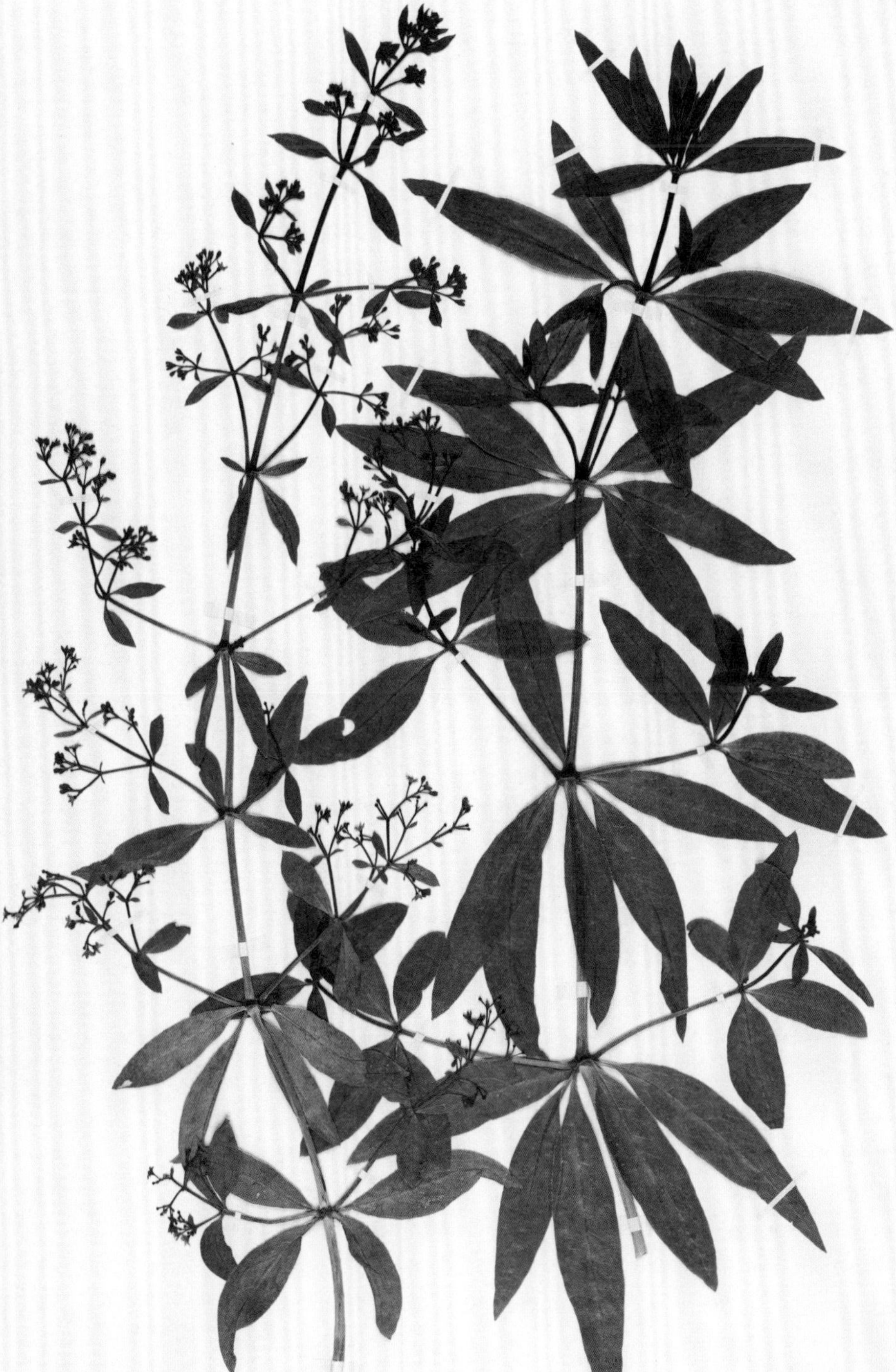

YINGPAN MAN MIGHT BE the world's best-dressed mummy. His caftan is remarkable: deep scarlet wool, woven with gold and lined with red silk. It's ornately patterned with fat nude puttis, or cherubs, pointing spears at pomegranates, while leaping goats and charging bulls are woven into repeating patterns below. Floral motifs swirl across his reddish-purple pants, and his feet are wrapped in silk and decorated with gold foil. In 1995, Yingpan Man was found in the Xinjiang Uyghur Autonomous Region of China. Situated in the northwest part of the country, near Kazakhstan and south of Mongolia, the region's remote location, dry climate, and freezing winters had kept Yingpan Man almost perfectly preserved. At around 3,000 km inland from the sea and notable for its hostile climate, archaeologists believe the region was one of the last places to be settled by humans.

During Yingpan Man's life (sometime around 300 CE), the region was a stop along the newly formed Silk Road. That he made the most of living on a trade route is clear from his burial garb. His style is international, combining classical Greek motifs like cherubs and laurel leaves with Persian and Chinese ones. He has pearls from coastal regions thousands of kilometers away, and a white hemp death mask that researchers have speculated might be related to the Tashtyk culture in Siberia—3,000 km northeast of his burial place. He is also decked out in gold, silk, and wool that were all likely traded. But the dyes used to make his scarlet robe are local. Analysis shows that his caftan was dyed with the plant species *Rubia cordifolia*, or common madder, and *Rubia tinctorum*, or dyer's madder.

Like woad and weld, nothing about the madder plant's above-ground appearance indicates that it is a dye plant. It is a hardy herb that flourishes in marshy wet soil; its lemon-yellow (not red) flowers are nestled among small, pointed leaves. But the lumpy orange-red roots of the dyer's madder plant betray it as a source of red dye. Gnarled like the fingers of a fairy tale witch, the twisted roots could be said to possess a kind of color-magic, producing a strikingly wide and diverse palette of reds. In skilled hands, madder roots create deep, permanent crimsons like those on Yingpan Man's caftan. With less expertise, brick reds and watermelon pinks emerge from the dye pot instead. Native to the eastern Mediterranean and Central Asia, dyer's madder is the most colorfast and widely used plant-based red dye, and it comes from a range of plants in the Rubiaceae family, the fifth-largest family of plants in the world.

While dyer's madder is the most common, several species are called madder. For example, wild madder (*Rubia peregrina*) has been used at least since the days of Pliny the Elder and Dioscorides in the first century CE; it grows wild across Europe and as far east as Iran. Indian madder, or munjeet (*Rubia cordifolia*), contains less alizarin—the colorant responsible for the red dye—but skillful dyers across the subcontinent have used it to create reds from poppies to burgundies. The Naga people of northeast India are renowned for their ember-like reds produced by a species now known as Naga madder (*Rubia sikkimensis*). Splendid cloaks found at the Paracas Necropolis in Peru dating from 2500 to 2250 BCE were dyed with South American Madder (*Relbunium ciliatum*). Lady's bedstraw (*Galium verum*) was the madder used for Scottish tartans. In the 17th century, lady's bedstraw was so popular that on the Hebridean islands of Harris and Lewis, famed for their tartans and tweeds, the machair, ancient communal pastures, were picked bare. Soon after, the pulling of *Galium* roots became punishable by death.

For centuries, madder was a reliable source of red dye that was both more readily available and cheaper than those made from insects like kermes and cochineal (more on those later). Along with woad and weld, madder formed the "grand teint"—the three dyes prized in medieval Europe for their strong, permanent primary colors.

Growing madder is a game of patience. It takes two to five years for the roots to grow large enough to be of any use as a dyestuff. While madder plants grow, they have often served as fodder for grazing animals, tinting sheep and cow's milk rose-pink. According to some sources, snacking on madder plants will dye a calf's bones, leaving red and white patterns like a candy cane.

The colorants in madder are anthraquinones, a class of organic compounds that contains all the most potent natural red dyes. Among the 15 anthraquinones in madder that play a role in dyeing, alizarin is the primary colorant and was the first dye to be successfully isolated and synthesized in 1868—a story we'll get to later. Purpurin is the second most-famous madder colorant, giving the plant a rosy hue, and there are pseudopurpurin, rubiadin, munjistin, etc. Each colorant adds its own tint and properties to the depth and range of dyer's madder.

↑ A young Norwegian woman wearing a folk dress poses in a photographic studio. Traditional Norwegian embroidery might feature wool dyed from *krapp* (madder), 1901.

Though madder roots can be used as a dyestuff when they're fresh, they are often dried, peeled, and powdered—a process that extends their shelf life and makes them easier to transport. From there, recipes for madder dyeing vary, but they all have some steps in common. To make a madder dye, first you soak the roots in cold water overnight (powdered, or chopped finely if they are fresh), then strain them out. The cloth to be dyed should be mordanted (pretreated with metal salts to increase the permanence and brightness of the dye), then added to the cold dye pot. Slowly warm the dye bath, being careful not to boil it; too much heat can transform the reds into dusty browns as some of the darker colorants in madder become more soluble at higher temperatures and overpower the red ones. Finally, several recipes recommend adding chalk (calcium carbonate) or passing the cloth through a solution of wheat bran and water to achieve the brightest reds.

Dyeing with madder goes back at least 5,000 years—the oldest known samples are from Mohenjo-daro, an ancient civilization in the Indus Valley, now Pakistan. These are tiny fragments of purple cloth that once wrapped a silver perfume jar and salt cellar, dating from around 3,000 BCE.

During its long tenure as a dyestuff, madder has developed an association with the military, from the battle dress of the Romans to the English red coats—the crimson jackets that were once the signature of the English army. In ancient Greece, Spartans used to dye their clothes red to hide bloodstains, and Napoleon mandated its use across his officers' uniforms. *Rubia tinctorum* has been used medicinally, too. One 16th-century account recommends using madder for bruises and wounds. The famous English physician Nicholas Culpeper prescribed its use for jaundice, palsy, sciatica, hemorrhoids, and getting rid of freckles.

Although it is the most important source of plant-based red, madder has long played second fiddle to the dyes created with scale insects, a family of small bugs with shield-like coatings, like cochineal and kermes, which produce brighter dyes more easily than madder. And since deep, saturated reds have long been associated with wealth and power (due in part to the considerable labor and skill that goes into making them), at times the competition between dyers using madder-based reds and those using insect-based ones has reached extremes. In 1255 scarlet dyers in the Italian city-state of Lucca drew up a guild statute forbidding the purchase of *radicem tingendi*, or "roots for dyeing"—likely madder. At the time, madder was less expensive than kermes, producing weaker scarlet "knock-offs." Dyers caught using madder had a choice of punishment: pay a fine of 1,000 lire (enough to buy a small farm) or lose a hand.

Although madder-dyed fabrics often lack the intense brightness of cloth dyed with insects, there is one exception. Turkey red is a colorfast, vibrant ruby named after the region where, between the 15th and 18th centuries, the secret recipe for the dye was held. It was also called Adrianople red for a city (now Edirne) that was a center of its production, and Levant red, a more general geographic reference to the eastern Mediterranean (now Israel, Jordan, Lebanon, and Syria). To protect their booming industry, Turkey red manufacturers kept their processes close to their chest, while dyers in western Europe clamored to get in on the action.

English and French textile firms sent industrial spies to the region who sometimes spent years studying and recording the process. But even after written recipes became widely available in western Europe in the 1740s, their fabrics continued to look dull and brickish by comparison. Making Turkey red was so delicate and complicated that it took years of further research and experimentation to come close to the desired bright-red results. To side-step this learning curve, some firms brought over master dyers from Greece and Turkey, endeavoring to learn directly from the source. Recipes vary but all the processes are arduous, including one that was detailed in an 1871 issue of *Scientific American*, which includes 11 operations. First, yarns are soaked in weak soda lye, then rinsed in a river. Next, sheep dung is plunged into a soda solution, mixed with olive oil, strained, and then combed through the yarn so that "no large lumps accumulate." This last step is key—the larger the sheep dung/olive oil lump, the more likely it is that the mixture will catch fire.

After the yarn dries, the lengthy procedure is to be repeated two to four times, depending on the strength of color desired. The process is rounded out by 13–20 steps (depending on the recipe), taking at least three weeks, demanding strenuous physical labor, and calling for a long list of ingredients—aside from olive oil and dung—including soda, ground oak galls, sumac, alum, tin crystals, nitric acid, and 50 pounds of beef blood (in Turkey the blood was more likely to come from sheep or goats).

The process is a pungent one. When Félix Beaujour, the French consul in Thessaloniki from 1794 to 1800, explored the small Greek village of Ampelakia, a center of Turkey red production, he was horrified by the overwhelming smell of the dye process. The stench was reportedly so putrid that the only inhabitants of Ampelakia were the dyers and their families—apparently no one else could stand the stink.

In the mid-19th century there was a short-lived madder boom. The price of cotton plummeted internationally due to increased mechanization, advances in dyes, and access to enslaved labor in the American South. Demand for cotton spiked as prices fell, and the demand for madder, a popular dye for cotton, climbed along with it. Huge industries in the Netherlands and France blossomed. But madder's success was cut short when alizarin, its main colorant, became the first natural dye to be synthesized, in 1868.

From that point on, only a few stalwarts stuck to using natural madder, including the famous British textile designer William Morris, who continued to use madder in his Merton Abbey workshop in southwest London—with mixed results. In 1903, the Persian government banned the importation of synthetic dyes, and Persian carpets became the last bastion of the madder industry; a severe law stated that dyers found using synthetic dyes would have their right hand cut off. But according to G. G. Lewis, an American rug expert, this was not strictly enforced—"else there would be at the present time—1920—many one-handed men in Persia."

A Recipe for *Adrianopole* Red

Adapted from *The Art of Dyeing Wool, Silk, and Cotton*, by Jean Hellot, Pierre Joseph Macquer, and Le Pileur d'Apligny (1785) (English translation 1901). This whopper of a recipe explains the intricacies of dyeing cotton the bright, candy-apple red you can achieve with madder (see page 74).

If you have 100 pounds of cotton to dye, put 150 pounds of Alicant soda (aka soda ash or sodium carbonate) wrapped in clean linen into a tub. This tub should have holes in the bottom so that the liquor may run into another tub underneath.

Cover the 150 pounds of soda in the upper tub with 300 quarts of river water, measured by wooden pails each containing 25 quarts. The water that passes from the first tub into the second should be taken out and poured over the soda again and again until it has extracted all of the salt.

You can test that this has worked using some oil: if the solution uniformly whitens and mixes well with the oil without any appearance of separation at the surface, it's sufficiently saturated with salt (you can use a fresh egg to test this if you're out of oil). Once the first batch is done, get another 300 quarts of river water, and repeat the process, this time using 150 pounds of fresh wood ashes instead of Alicant soda. Repeat the process a third time, but this time use 75 pounds of quicklime instead of wood ashes.

Next, add 100 pounds of cotton to a tub, then add an equal quantity of each of the solutions you've just made: the Alicant soda, the wood ashes, and the quicklime. Don't use the full volume you've made, just enough to get the fabric wet, putting the rest aside for later. Stir together until the fabric is fully saturated. Then put into a copper pot full of water (don't wring it out, it should be dripping wet) and boil it for three hours. Take it out and wash it in running water, then air dry it.

Mix 133 quarts of each of your solutions (soda, wood ash, quicklime) so you have a big bath of around 400 quarts total. Add 25 pounds of sheep's dung with some juice from sheep intestines to this mix and stir with a wooden pestle. Strain the whole thing through a fine sieve. Add 12.5 pounds of good olive oil to the mix, which should form a soapy liquor.

Dip the cotton you'd like to dye in this mix (this should be pre-mordanted with alum), stirring every time. Leave the cotton in for 12 hours, then take it out and dry it. Repeat this three times. Catch the liquor that drips from the cotton in a trough—this is called *sickiou* and we'll use it later to brighten the dye.

After you've dipped the cotton three times in your sheep's dung mix, make another solution the same as the first (400 quarts of equal parts soda solution, wood ash solution, and quicklime solution). Leave out the sheep's dung this time, but don't forget the olive oil! Repeat the same three processes (leaving in for 12 hours and drying between) as you did the first time. When you're done that, carefully wash your cotton in the river to get all the oil off, and it should be as white as if it had been bleached.

When dry, mordant the cotton twice with alum. First, pulverize about a quarter pound of oak galls for every pound of cotton. The first time, use six ounces of alum, and six ounces of your now-beloved soda–wood ash–quicklime mix. Then wait three to four days and repeat the process, this time using four ounces of each.

Wait a few days and you're (finally) ready to make your dye. Dissolve two pounds of powdered madder in water for every pound of cotton. Before you dye, add 20 pounds of sheep's blood. Then skim the rising scum off the top of your dye.

Prep the cotton (again) by adding it to a pot of wood ashes that have been dissolved in the best white Marseilles soap and warm water. Add 100 pounds of cotton, and work it until the fiber is saturated.

Add 600 quarts of water and your madder–sheep's blood solution to a copper pot and heat it. Add the cotton, and boil for six hours over a very slow fire as evenly as possible. Cover the liquid so no vapors escape. When that is done, wash and dry the fiber immediately. Then soak it in the sickiou you saved from earlier for an hour. Wring it out and air dry.

When dry, dissolve five pounds of soap for every 100 pounds of cotton in enough water to cover the cotton. Heat the water until it's warm, and then add this to a copper pot filled with 600 quarts of water. Boil this gently for four to five hours, keeping the copper pot covered. According to the author, you should now have a red "much brighter than the finest Adrianopole carnation."

Safflower

Carthamus tinctorius

Kingdom. Plantae

Order. Asterales

Family. Asteraceae

Other name. Bastard saffron

Primary colorants. Flavanoids, carthamin

Colors. Safflower produces two different dyes, a yellow one and a red one

Fastness. *Yellow:* poor, *red:* good

Type of dye. *Yellow:* mordant/adjective, *red:* none

MENTION THE PHRASE "RED TAPE" and it will send chills down the spines of civil servants around the globe. The expression today summons a tangled web of bureaucracy, but the expression "red tape" was once used to indicate the urgency of a letter. In 16th-century Spain, a bright red ribbon was tied around important documents to mark them as top priority. Red symbolized wealth and power, and undyed ribbons were used to wrap less critical documents. Soon, other governments started copying the practice. When the English king Henry VIII lobbied Pope Clement VII to annul his marriage to Catherine of Aragon in 1530, he sent 80 petitions wrapped in poppy-red ribbon. The English legal system picked up the color-coding too, and to this day the country's barristers still use red ribbon to bundle court briefs together.

The red dye that gives its color to all that bureaucracy is derived from a plant called safflower, or bastard saffron. Safflower is the domesticated version of a plant native to North India that has been cultivated in areas around the Mediterranean for millennia. It is a herb with dark, toothed leaves and flaming orange flowers that have a tuft of spiky petals, like a thistle crossed with a marigold. Safflower is included in this book because of its long, contentious history as both a knockoff and a prestigious dye in its own right. As a dyestuff, safflower is unique. While all dye plants have multiple colorants, no other dye plant has colorants that work like safflower's. It produces two different dyes from the petals of the plant; one ranges from lemon yellow to apricot, and the other—which can only be extracted after the lemon yellow dye has been washed away—dyes fabric coral pinks to tawny reds.

Safflower's slim orange petals have earned it the nickname "bastard saffron" because they look like the stigmas (the part of the flower that collects pollen) of the more expensive plant, saffron. Safflower petals are dead ringers for saffron stigmas, but while each saffron crocus has just three tiny stigmas jutting from a lilac flower, the safflower is a pompom of dozens of petals.

Due in part to how complicated it is to harvest (each stigma must be hand-picked), the wispy orange stigmas of the saffron flower have been the costliest spice globally for around three millennia. In the ancient world it was also a prestigious dyestuff; vast amounts of saffron are required to make even a little dye, which elevated its golden hues into the wardrobes of royalty. And while it may be dazzling as a color, saffron isn't that stable—over time it fades from egg-yolk yellow to buttery blond.

Safflower petals make two different colors; one is a citrusy yellow and the other is a pinkish red that can only be coaxed from the petals once all of the yellow dye has been washed out. To get safflower's yellow dye is comparatively simple. To start, pluck the slim orange petals at the height of the season, then soak them in cold water (the more safflower petals, the stronger the color). The golden dye will leech out of the petals into the water, and the resulting liquid can be strained and then gently heated before dyers add fiber or cloth to the pot. But safflower's yellow is fugitive—meaning it fades with exposure to light and washing—so this process is more often performed as a stepping stone to get the red. One medieval Venetian source recommends putting the petals in a cloth bag and leaving them in a gently running river overnight to wash out the yellow dye. A later 18th-century French source suggests trampling the flowers before soaking them to make the yellow rinse out more quickly.

Once you've drained the safflower petals of their yellow dye, another process is required to reach red. First an alkaline—a substance with a high pH—like soda ash (sodium carbonate) or pearl ash (potassium carbonate) is added to cold water with the damp flowers. Then the mixture is stirred and left to sit for five or six hours. Next, the flowers are strained out and an acidic liquid is added. Recipes for this step call for everything from lemon juice to vinegar, to a decoction of green mangoes, or a sour broth of unripe pomegranates cooked with millet. This is called *virer le bain* in French, or "turning the bath." As the mixture shifts from alkaline to acid, the plant's red colorant, called carthamin, precipitates out and becomes a usable dye.

Despite its limitations, sometimes the yellow dye is the main act: pale yellow bandages dyed with safflower wrap an Egyptian mummy from the 12th Dynasty (*c.*1938–1756 BCE), protected from exposure to the elements for 4,000 years and so still a sunny, mellow yellow. In China, safflower yellow was used as an underdye for scarlet, and in India as an underdye for indigo.

↓ A safflower is drawn with a quote from the poet Onono Komachi from the *Kokin Wakashū* (Collection of Japanese Poems of Ancient and Modern Times). Lip rouge named komachi-beni started to be sold in the late 19th century

↗ Rinsing the petals to abstract the yellow pigment to make beni rouge, 1912–1923

→ Safflowers increase in redness after the washing and fermentation process, 1912–1923

↘ Rolling the paste used to make benimochi petal disks, 1912–1923

Unlike most other dyes, safflower reds will work on fabrics without a mordant, and while they're fairly colorfast, even this dye isn't as stable as others like indigo or madder. For example, a 16th-century fragment of a Persian velvet tent panel features an illustrative weave of a well-muscled warrior hunting a lion. Both the warrior's tunic and his horse were dyed with safflower red mixed with indigo, and both now have a strange greenish pallor. Researchers believe the fabric started out dark purple and brown, but that the safflower dye mutated over time, turning to faded turquoise.

The trade and use of safflower was introduced to China sometime around the third century CE, where it was called *hong hua*, meaning red flower, or *honglan*, meaning red indigo. It was used to dye silks the color of sunsets and as a cosmetic to rouge cheeks. Buddhist monks in the prosperous city of Dunhuang made detailed records of its cultivation and sale.

In Japan, safflower is called *benibana*, and is a prestigious color long associated with money. One proverb, "ikko ichigon," translates as "a pound of beni is worth a pound of gold." Since the eighth century CE, *ootan*, a color that is a blend of safflower red and gardenia yellow, has been reserved for the crown prince, and until the 20th century, dyers used safflower to create the red rising sun on the Japanese flag. The plant has also been connected to blood circulation, especially menstruation, and from the Heian period (794–1185 CE) fabrics dyed with safflower were worn next to the skin in order to facilitate spiritual and physical healing.

Safflower is famous for its use as a cosmetic, too. In Japan, *beni* reddened the lips of famous geishas and blushed the cheeks of empresses. In China, the name *yanzhi*, for safflower, is still used as a word for makeup. Powdered safflower pigment mixed with talc was a favorite rouge of many European women, who called it "Spanish vermilion." Advising women on their complexion, the 1825 British guide *The Art of Beauty* suggests rouge "rendered extremely innocently." Safflower is on its list of preferred ingredients and is still used in cosmetics today. Even though carthamin, the main colorant in safflower's red dye, was only successfully synthesized in 2019, the use of safflower as a dye declined steeply over the course of the 20th century, thanks to a range of other synthetic red competitors.

But another part of the safflower plant remains commercially useful. The seeds can be pressed into a thick oil, which, as well as being added to paint and hair-care products, is a popular cooking oil found in kitchens everywhere.

In ancient Assyria, safflower had yet another use. Shepherds smeared the pigment on the genitals of rams so they could tell which ewes had been mounted—they just had to count the pink-stained bottoms.

→ Safflower
(*Carthamus tinctorius*)

95 To Dye Thread, Yarn or Linen Cloth a *Sad Brown*

This recipe is adapted from the medieval book of secrets, *The Secrets of Alexis: Containing Many Excellent Remedies against Diverse Diseases, Wounds and Other Accidents* (1615).

To turn linen a sad brown, procure a pound of bastard saffron and travel to the banks of a river that is flowing with some speed. Once there, put the bastard saffron petals in a little cloth bag, then hang it in the river water for a day and a night (you may need to find some string and a big tree branch to tie the bag to, or resign yourself to standing vigil). Over the hours the petals will leach out a yellow dye. But Alexis doesn't want this yellow liquid and neither do we. Continue the river rinse until the water flowing over and through your bag of bastard saffron runs clear. Then we're instructed to add a rank (whatever that is) of bastard saffron in a pot that's not too thick, add a rewe (whatever that is) of bastard saffron, and a rewe of ashes, and cover it all with water, sealing the pot with a lid.

Let the mixture stand for seven or eight hours. Keep the solution and strain out the bastard saffron and ashes into a long, triangular cloth bag with a sharp point at the bottom. Add eight pots of water and four pots of vinegar. Strain the solution through the bag of saffron 15 or 16 times. This mixture is "the first dyeing of color," or the first extraction of the colorants, which is usually the richest and brightest (or in this case, saddest and brownest). Set this to one side. For the "second dyeing of color," strain the same amount of water and vinegar through your bag 15 more times, and you'll get a paler dye. Repeat this process one more time for the "third dyeing."

You're finally ready to make some sad brown linen. Heat up your first dyeing of color. Add your thread or linen cloth, leaving it in the mixture for a night. Then hang it up without wringing or rubbing it. Repeat, using the same fabric with the second dyeing and then with the third, this time letting the fabric steep in the bastard saffron liquid for seven hours each time.

Weld

Reseda luteola

Kingdom. Plantae

Order. Brassicales

Family. Resedaceae

Other names. Dyer's mignonette, dyer's rocket, dyer's weed, gualda

Primary colorants. Flavonoids: luteolin, apignen, luteolin methylether

Colors. Yellows

Fastness. Good

Mordant. Alum, iron

THE WELD PLANT, *RESEDA LUTEOLA*, looks like something Dr. Seuss would invent. Tall, feathery yellow flowers sprout from a central rosette (a cluster of narrow leaves at the plant's base) and lean dramatically, stooping and twisting in the wind. Alongside saffron, sawwort, and dyer's broom, weld is one of the most common plant sources of yellow dye.

On its own, weld's palette spans from pale straw to bright Amalfi lemon. When mixed with woad or indigo, it makes grassy and leafy greens. Coptic Egyptian dyers from the third to the 10th century used weld to make orange (with madder) and green (with woad or indigo). In Nubia (modern Sudan), khakis and olives from the first six centuries CE are weld mixed with an iron mordant, while one 18th-century French dyer's notebook lists an expansive palette dyed with weld: golden yellow, yellow wax, hazelnut, dead leaf, tobacco, and rotten olive.

Weld produces beautiful dyes and has been widely used for centuries across the globe, but it's never achieved the lofty reputation afforded some of the other dye plants explored in this book. If indigo is the king of natural dyes, weld is a country duke—mostly respected, but a little provincial and the subject of derision; anyone could do weld's job. This is because weld dyes yellow, which has an abundance of sources. There's an old saying that dates from medieval Florentine dyers: *ogni erbaccia fa tinta*—"any weed can give a dye"—and those dyes are nearly always creams, lemons, ambers, and other shades of yellow. While true-blue dyes, deep purples, and rich reds are scarce, yellow dye plants are a dime a dozen. So weld—while dependable and widely used—has never reached the industrial scale of madder or the elite status of indigo.

Weld's superiority over other yellow dyes is for its fastness—its ability to stay bright and vibrant over time. Alongside woad and madder, it formed the aforementioned "grand teint," the Medieval triad of fast, go-to primary-colored dyes. And while weld is the fastest—or most permanent—yellow, it's got nothing on the permanence of blues and reds. There are no naturally occurring yellow colorants that have the staying power of indigotin or alizarin. So, medieval tapestries often get "the blues," meaning the sections that were once green—meadows, fields, farms—turn aquamarine over time. These green sections were usually dyed with woad and weld, and while the weld yellows fade over time, the woad blues remain, causing some medieval tapestries to look like they are set underwater.

With few exceptions, the colorants in yellow dyes are flavonoids, which is a catch-all term for a huge class of compounds with the same basic chemical structure. They're *secondary metabolites*, which means the small flavonoid molecules don't directly play a role in plant growth, development, or reproduction. Instead, they have a wide range of supporting roles: making flowers smell good, defending against frost and drought, and, crucially, providing color.

There are over 5,000 flavonoids in fruits and vegetables like strawberries, grapes, and kale, and some of them produce the hues that let us know a piece of fruit is ripe and delicious. Flavonoids transform bell peppers from mossy greens to fire-engine reds as they ripen. Likewise, they transform leaves from springtime green to red-orange in autumn; they are responsible for the reds of rose petals, and the sunny yellows of daffodils. Although flavonoids bring plenty of color to the botanical world, only a few of them make decent dyes for textiles.

The main flavonoid responsible for weld's yellow dye is called luteolin. There are also small amounts of another flavonoid, apigenin, and traces of a third, luteolin methylether. Of the three colorants, luteolin is the most lightfast—it is responsible for weld's relative permanence in comparison with other yellow flavonoid dyes. It's also present in the greatest quantities, though the exact concentrations of colorants found in weld depend on growing conditions and when it's harvested, which in turn affect the color of the dye and its performance over time.

Canary yellows can be coaxed from weld with a (comparatively) simple process. The first step is mordanting the fabric—all flavonoid dyes require the use of mordants, the metal salts that form a chemical bridge between the dye and the cloth fibers. Without a mordant, the yellows achieved with weld will quickly turn a pallid shade of beige.

Next, you'll want to toss fresh, frozen, or dried weld into the dye pot (dried weld gives a weaker color, so you need more of it), and cover the

plants with boiling water (you can use the whole plant to dye but there are more colorants concentrated in the flowers, young stems, and leaves than in older stems and roots). Let the weld sit in the water overnight, and in the morning, add a little more water and gently heat. Strain out the soggy remnants of the weld plant, then add your cloth to the pot and let it steep for an hour or more.

While there's no doubt that weld has been one of the most popular dyes for millennia, tracing its use through history is more difficult than it is for other dyes because of the nature of flavonoids. Most other dyes have a distinct chemical fingerprint—indigotin only comes from indigo-producing plants, for example, and carminic acid only comes from cochineal—but weld contains the same colorants as many other yellow-producing dye plants. Saw-wort and dyer's broom contain hefty amounts of luteolin and apigenin, for instance, and so do less-used dyestuffs like dandelion and weedy yarrow.

Then there's the already-stated fact that yellow dyes degrade faster than their red and blue counterparts. So, when conservators, historians, or archaeologists try to analyze yellow dyes through quantitative methods (like the previously introduced HPLC), they hit a brick wall. The yellow dyes are often so degraded that they produce misleading results, or reveal colorants that could have as easily come from weld as they could from other sources of yellow dye.

So in order to reconstruct the story of weld, historians and archaeologists have figured out a few different ways to fill in the gaps. First, they align the dye with written sources; weld makes an appearance in the writings of Pliny, Vitruvius, and Virgil, so we know it was used in ancient Rome. The Latin manuscript the *Mappae Clavicula* (a book of formulas for substances used in crafts and a medieval precursor to the modern how-to guide) includes multiple recipes for dyeing with weld, including one that calls for "the dung of a dog, a dove, and a cock." Later Florentine and Venetian books of secrets—eclectic instructions for everything from love potions to stain removers—contain recipes for overdyeing weld with indigo and using it with tannins to create tawny browns. Finally, a series of 18th-century treatises on dyeing from Spain and France prove that weld was used on an industrial scale. Complementing these recipe books are

← The pale yellow flowers of weld growing in rural Cornwall, England, 1964

records from company accounts and trade guilds, as well as tax records that provide further insight into the historical use of weld.

Ancillary evidence, like seeds, can also tell us about the plants that were used for dyeing. For instance, weld seeds were found during the excavation of Neolithic sites on several Swiss lakes—Pfäffikon, Zurich, and Neuchâtel—which points to an early textile industry. Basically, if there are high concentrations of weld seed around, people were likely dyeing with it since weld isn't very tasty. Still, confirming the ingredients used in historical samples of yellow cloth requires some serious detective work.

From records we do have, it's clear that from the Middle Ages to the late 18th century, weld reigned supreme as the pre-eminent yellow dye in Europe, but like woad, its popularity was supplanted by an imported dyestuff. In 1775, chemist Edward Bancroft introduced a new yellow dye to Europe called quercitron, which comes from the inner bark of a North American oak tree and is buttery, warm, and golden. As Thomas Cooper, a chemistry professor and printer, put it in 1815, quercitron was "good, permanent and cheap," though "not quite so bright and not quite so permanent however as weld." Despite the implied inferiority—which Bancroft, as the dye's importer, naturally disputed—quercitron had a few practical advantages over weld. It dyed fabric at lower temperatures, saving energy and time. It was also easier to use in printing calicos and chintzes—brightly colored, intricately patterned cotton fabrics that originated in India, but that were fashionable across Europe and North America in Bancroft's day. In the years after it was introduced, quercitron became the preferred option for making these prints for the wider fashion market, knocking weld off its golden pedestal. Now, neither dye is used commercially, though weld is a popular choice for craft dyers and hobbyists.

↓ Yarn simmers in dye
warming over an open fire
near Östersund, Sweden, 1964

FAUNA

Cochineal
Kermes
Lac
Murex

We often overlook what is around us. Especially when what is around is small and a little gross; namely those multilimbed, creepy, crawly, squirming insects that many of us (excluding entomologists and curious children) go out of our way to avoid. But there is no avoiding them here: bugs are the source of some of the world's most enduring and valuable red dyes.

Dyes from animals are rarer than plant dyes, and they are also more prestigious, making some of the most rich, permanent colors in the world. Dyers across the globe have long used an extended family of legless scale insects, the Coccidae, to create stunning, permanent scarlets. The most well known is a South American bug, *Cochineal*, which turned the dye industry on its head when Spain began importing the dried insects into Europe. Then, there is *Kermes*, the source of Venetian scarlet, a color so lauded that at one point anyone trying to copy it lost their right hand. Third, there's the *Lac* insect, a bug found in India, Thailand, and Vietnam, as famous for its natural

resin, shellac, as for its illustrious red dye. To top off this section, a family of carnivorous sea snails, which were the source of the single most treasured dye in the ancient Mediterranean, *Murex*.

Cochineal

Dactylopius coccus

Kingdom. Metazoa

Order. Hemiptera

Superfamily. Coccoidea

Family. Dactylopiidae

Other names. American cochineal, true cochineal

Primary colorant. Carminic acid

Colors. Reds

Fastness. Excellent

Type of dye. Mordant/adjective

COCHINEAL IS THE WORLD'S most prestigious natural red dye. It's a permanent, deep crimson that comes from a parasitic insect of the same name, found across South and Central America. A few other red-dye-producing bugs are called cochineal: there is Polish cochineal (*Porphyrophora polonica*) (which also goes by the ominous moniker Saint John's Blood) and Armenian cochineal (*Porphyrophora hamelii*), but the insect from the Americas is the most famous and potent of them all. It was so valuable in the Mesoamerican world that the Aztec emperor Moctezuma demanded it as tribute. A century later, cochineal had become so popular in Europe that the French monarch Louis XIV, known as the "Sun King" and the mastermind behind the famous palace at Versailles, ordered that his new chairs and royal bed curtains be dyed with cochineal. The little bugs were the second most valuable export from the Spanish American colonies, after silver (and more profitable than gold).

The use of cochineal goes far back in time. In 1927, Peruvian archaeologists Julio C. Tello and Toribio Mejía Xesspe began excavating the Paracas necropolis, an ancient burial ground on Peru's south coast dating from between 300 BCE and 200 CE. Their team uncovered 429 funerary bundles—mummies swaddled in as many as 60 layers of cloth, with food, pigments, ornaments, and even weapons enclosed between the layers—everything the deceased wanted to take with them to the afterlife.

The bundles' outer layers are rough cotton, but underneath the simple exteriors they found vividly dyed, intricately patterned mantles, woven rectangles of fabric enveloping the mummy. The mantles are a mix of camelid (alpaca, llama, guanaco, or vicuña) fibers and cotton. Some feature simple geometric designs, others are elaborately embroidered recountings of myths with large, central protagonist figures, and still others show intricate details stitched into repeating scenes. But they all have one thing in common: the fabrics are, 2,000 years later, still brightly colored, from leafy greens to cobalt blues, vermilion reds to rich golds, pure whites to inky blacks. The evidence is clear—the ancient people of Paracas were a dab hand with dyes.

In the 1960s, chemist Max Saltzman analyzed the mantles' dyes using high-performance liquid chromatography (HPLC), a technique that involves dissolving a sample of the dye in a solvent and then measuring the spectrum of light it absorbs. Each colorant has a unique pattern of light absorption, so even dyes that might appear similar to the naked eye—like reds made with cochineal and madder—can be differentiated. Saltzman found that while some of the red textiles from Paracas were dyed with plants related to madder, the samples also contained the first known example of cochineal dye—a sprightly 2,000 years young and still bright red.

Cochineal is best known for its bright red dyes, though it can produce a vibrant spectrum of warm colors that range from delicate pinks through to tangerine oranges and the bloodiest scarlets. Cochineal recipes from the 18th century span from plum gray, which is a washed-out purple, to *soupe au vin* (wine soup), a color somewhere between burgundy and black that is made by dyeing with cochineal on a fabric already dyed blue. To make *langouste*, a color that matches the fiery vermilion of a cooked lobster, cochineal is dyed over a yellow dye known as young fustic, made from the wood of *Cotinus coggygria*, a small tree also called the smoketree or Venetian sumac. Dye manuals from that era contain a further host of evocative cochineal color names: flame scarlet, cherry red, jujube, daffodil, and lastly, a shade that matches the putty color of a schoolroom eraser (and no one's actual skin color)—flesh pink.

Cochineal is considered the best natural red dye in the world for a few reasons. The first is the depth and range of colors it supplies, which are not just beautiful but permanent. While you can make similar colors with other dyestuffs, it's a lot harder. Making Turkey red—the madder-based red so intense and striking that it precipitated centuries of industrial espionage—takes four weeks of complicated processing and an ingredient list that includes both goat's blood and dung. Getting identical hues from cochineal is much simpler; the same crimsons can be achieved in a day.

Another reason for cochineal's pre-eminence is the concentration of the primary colorant—carminic acid—in each insect. Weight for weight, you need a lot less American cochineal than any of the other red-producing scale insects to get the same shades. For example, to dye silk a deep scarlet you need between 12 and 15 percent of the silk's weight in cochineal. To get the same color with Armenian cochineal would require between 600 and 1,400 percent of the silk's weight in dried insects.

Cochineal has been an art stalwart, too. If you visit the Louvre in Paris or the Metropolitan Museum of Art in New York, you'd be hard pressed not to see its traces. The crimson and scarlet paints on canvases by some of the world's more revered painters were made from the little bugs. Colorants in the insects can be extracted and processed into carmine—a blue-red pigment that is one of the most stable and permanent in the world. Carmine pigment is suspended in a medium, usually linseed oil, to make it into an oil paint that's been used by the likes of Van Gogh, Caravaggio, Vermeer, and Rembrandt.

Each cochineal insect is small—about the size of a grain of rice—but they huddle together, making dusty, white clumps on the paddle-shaped, bristle-covered lobes of *Opuntia* cacti, commonly called nopals or prickly pears. The adult female insects are the source of the colorants, mostly carminic acid, which make up nearly a quarter of each insect's weight. Carminic acid is an anthraquinone, a category of organic compounds that make some of the best natural dyes. Alizarin and purpurin, the main colorants in madder, are anthraquinones, and so are the colorants in kermes and lac. Female cochineal are immobile, meaning once they've attached themselves to the cacti they spend the rest of their lives in the same spot, feeding off its sticky nectar. Their appearance, like fluffy cotton balls, is down to a whitish, waxy protective coating that encases their round, segmented bodies.

Even today, farmers harvest cochineal by hand. First, they brush the insects off the cacti (the tools for this have varied through history: feathers, brushes, sticks, or knives). Then they boil or steam the cochineal to kill them, and finally, they dry the insects on mats in the hot sun. Once dry, the shriveled cochineal insects look like red peppercorns, and it's in this form that they are ground into a fine powder and used to make a dye bath.

It takes about 70,000 dried cochineal bugs to produce a pound of dye powder—enough to dye 13 wool sweaters a bright cardinal red. To use cochineal as a dye, the dried, powdered bugs are covered with water and boiled, then strained and boiled again. This decanting process is repeated several times to reach a crimson dye. Then, the tone is adjusted; cochineal dye is pH sensitive, which means you can change the color of the dye bath by adding an acid or an alkali. For instance, if you add an acid like

↑ A view of a cochineal plantation taken during the voyage of HMS *Challenger*, 1872–1876

→ Cochineal scale on the leaves of prickly pear (*Opuntia ficus-india*), 1928

↓ Sharecroppers brushing cochineal scale from prickly pear at a cochineal plantation in Las Palmas, Gran Canaria

vinegar, it will turn a true, Santa-suit red. If you add an alkaline like soda ash (sodium carbonate), it will shift towards magenta. Adding iron will turn the bath dark purple.

Once the dye bath has cooled, the sweaters (or whatever you're dyeing) are added to the pot, and the whole mix is slowly heated up again. After an hour or so, the sweaters should be the scarlet or fuchsia you were aiming for. Then, the "exhaust bath" (a name for the weaker dye left over from the initial red bath) can be used to turn a dozen more sweaters pink.

Cochineal originated in South America, although whether its use began in Peru or another region is still contested. Many of the surviving pre-Columbian textiles are from Peru because of the dry climate in its coastal regions and the Andes. Almost none survive from the Mayan and Aztec empires further north in what is now Mexico, Guatemala, and Belize, as the warm, wet climates tend to break down fabrics over time. And while cochineal was used extensively by indigenous peoples as a dye, no recipes from the pre-Columbian era have been found. Instead, the hard evidence we have for cochineal use in the region comes from codices—historical manuscripts that are the ancestor of the modern book—and maps. The red inks in some codices are made from cochineal pigment; in others, the use of cochineal is illustrated—there are painted figures of the nopal cacti, drawings of red insects, and scenes of cochineal processing.

The most important codex is the 1511–1512 *Matricula de Tributos*, an inventory record from the Aztec Empire (in what is now central Mexico) documenting cochineal as a tribute, a payment made from one state to another as a sign of respect and dependence. As well as bags of cochineal, the *Matricula de Tributos* documents opulent scarlet cloaks and crimson feathered headpieces to be given to the emperor, all likely dyed with cochineal. From the early 1500s onwards, there are also official Spanish reports, surveys, scientific reports, trading records, and travelers' accounts.

While the origins of the pre-Columbian cochineal industry are uncertain, the *Matricula dos Tributos*, together with later evidence, shows that by the 16th century the highlands of Mixteca and Oaxaca in southwest Mexico had become its center—together the regions were responsible for a tribute of nearly 4,500 kg of cochineal annually. Though the bugs were found wild there, over time people began farming cochineal. We have no record of when this practice began, but by the time the Spanish conquered Tenochtitlan (now Mexico City) in 1521, there were well-established systems of farming and trade.

Farming cochineal proved to be hard work. Though the domesticated insects were bred to almost double the size of their wild cousins and produced more carminic acid, they came with their own set of problems. The farmed cochineal, though full of juicy red acid, were more susceptible than their forebears to changing weather patterns. The waxy white coating on their bodies was thinner and less protective, so a cold snap or heatwave could mean the end for the domesticated bugs. Clutches of pregnant females, known as *madres*, were kept inside the homes of farmers during the stormy season to protect them, or carried as far as 30 miles up into the mountains to pass the season in a drier region. The cacti that the cochineal clung to also required care; susceptible to frost and rot, these plants had to be kept clean and frequently pruned. Over time, the cochineal growers became custodians of the little legless bugs.

While cochineal was widely farmed and traded before the colonization of Mexico began in 1519, the Spanish intensified its production. The first shipment of cochineal to Europe was sent in 1523, and the dye's popularity steadily increased across the continent over the following decades. As a result of this demand, cochineal became a cash crop for Spain, which tried to keep the origins of the dyestuff a secret to hold their monopoly in place. By the mid-16th century, Spanish flotillas were ferrying huge shipments from its colonies (primarily in what is now Mexico) back to Europe. A century later, exports of dried cochineal insects were estimated at 350 tons per year—enough to dye almost 200,000 meters of wool fabric cherry red—and by the end of the 16th century, cochineal was being sold on a global scale, with trade networks established in the Middle East and Central Asia, as well as the Philippines and China.

By the 18th century, cochineal farming took the form of *haciendas*—huge plantations with 50,000 (or more) cacti growing at any given time. The Spanish initially set up these plantations in traditional cochineal-farming areas, but levels of production could not always be guaranteed.

When confronted by famines or epidemics, which weren't infrequent, farmers would abandon cochineal crops to grow maize in order to eat.

By the 19th century, Spain's empire was in decline, but the country held fast to its cochineal monopoly, despite repeated attempts by other world powers to break it. However, by 1825, Spain no longer had any colonies in mainland South America, and the newly independent nations of Mexico, Guatemala, Nicaragua, Honduras, and El Salvador each fostered their own cochineal industry. In reaction to the increased competition (and to try to cut its colonial losses), Spain introduced cochineal insects and the Mexican hacienda system to the Canary Islands, which quickly became a global center for cochineal production. In 1875, 2,722 tons of cochineal were harvested from the Canaries, enough to dye 6,000,976 wool sweaters fire-engine red.

The global market for cochineal, like other natural dyes, collapsed with the invention of synthetics in the late 19th century. These days, natural cochineal is produced on a small scale for craft dyers and artisans, and is used in the food and beauty industries. Known by its other name, E120, cochineal is processed into a food additive that gives us the ruby hues of red velvet cakes, cherry colas, and lipsticks the world over. So while natural cochineal is no longer used to dye the scarlet cloaks of emperors, E120 is a regular in your supermarket's deli aisle; it's the red that colors salamis and tinned fish, and behind the cosmetics counter it's the rosy tint of synthetic blush.

Kermes

Kermes vermilio

Kingdom. Metazoa

Order. Hemiptera

Superfamily. Coccoidea

Family. Kermesidae

Other name. Dyer's kermes

Primary colorant. Kermesic acid

Colors. Reds

Fastness. Excellent

Type of dye. Mordant/adjective

TAB. XXXVI.

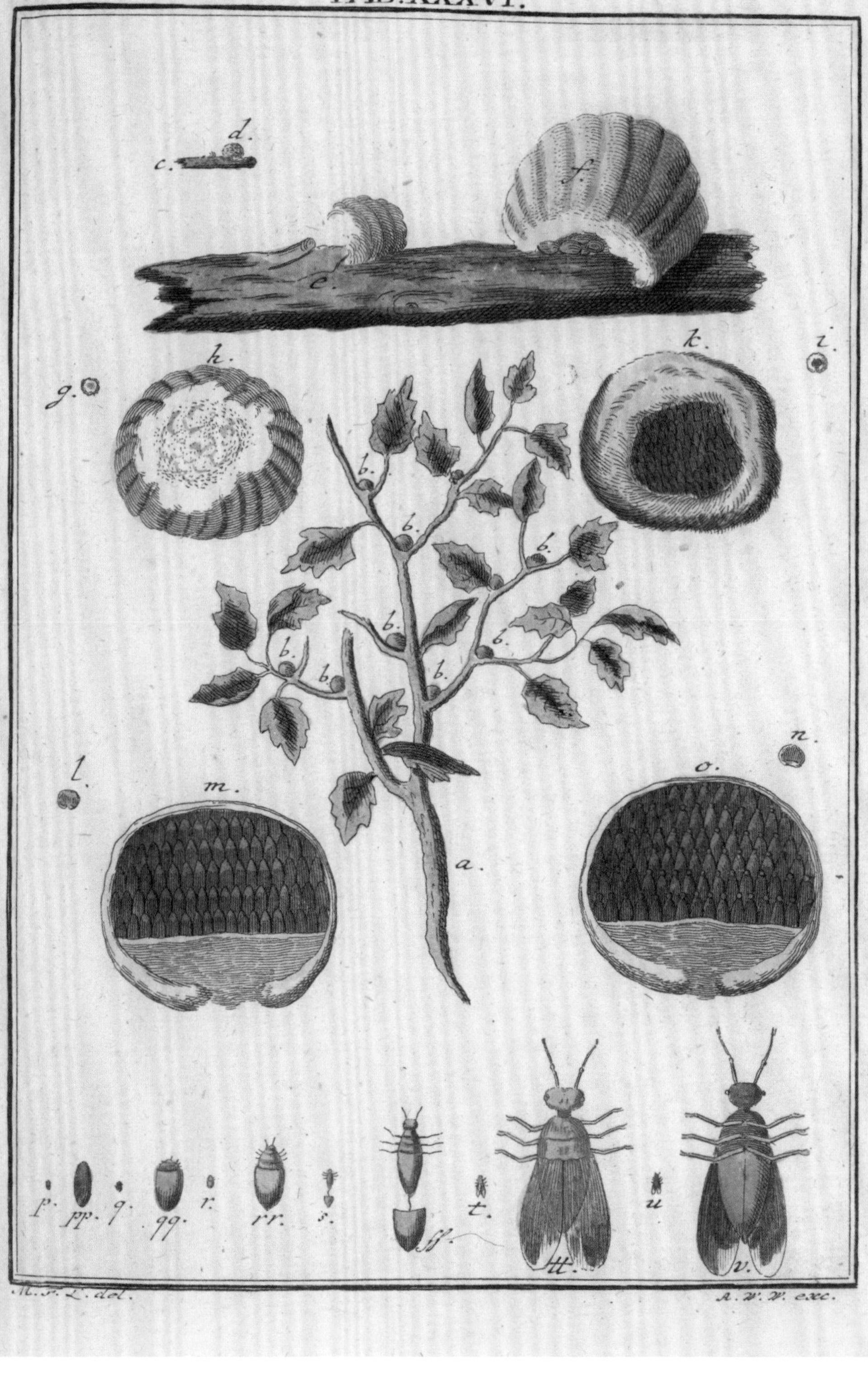

M. S. L. del. A. W. W. exc.

IN 275 CE THE KING OF PERSIA sent the Emperor Aurelius a gift that drove the Roman leader's court into a frenzy—a scarlet wool cloak that was brighter and more lustrous than any other ever seen, and not one of the dyers in Rome could tell Aurelius how the color had been made.

Not to be outdone, Aurelius embarked on a far-flung mission to find the color's source (or, at least, he sent other people on a far-flung mission). Aurelius commanded his master dyers to travel east to Persia and beyond to find the dye. They returned empty handed, some claiming it might be a new variety of madder, though none could say for sure.

Though some scholars still dispute the dyestuff that colored the scarlet cloak, it likely came from kermes (*Kermes vermilio*), a scale insect in the same family as cochineal. During the reign of Aurelius, Romans were familiar with kermes as a dye, but it seems they might not have had the technical skills to unlock its potential in the same way that the Persian dyers had done. Some of Aurelius' court dyers might even have suspected the origin of the scarlet cloak's color—but admitting that it was dyed with kermes meant confessing they couldn't match the skills of a rival foreign power, so they would likely have kept their mouths shut.

Kermes are parasites that appear on certain kinds of oak trees. The bulbous bodies of the adult females—full of unlaid eggs—are the source of a red dye that was the most illustrious and lauded throughout the Middle East, North Africa, and Europe until the Spanish introduced cochineal from South America into Europe in the 16th century (see page 108).

Kermes and cochineal have a lot in common; they're in the same extended family of scale insects—small bugs with shield-like coverings—and they both create permanent dyes that range from pinks to oranges to dark reds. But while kermes and cochineal have similar colorants (kermesic acid and carminic acid, respectively), cochineal contains greater concentrations of its colorant than kermes does, which means you need less of it to dye the same colors. In addition, cochineal can be farmed, while kermes have proved impossible to cultivate commercially. It therefore comes as no surprise that when the Spanish started to import cochineal into Europe it knocked kermes from the top spot.

↙ Harald Böhmer and Dominique Cardon looking for kermes lice in Turkey, 1989

↓ Female insects filled with larvae are collected and killed in vinegar, before being dried to be used as a dye, Turkey, 1989

Still, kermes had thousands of years in the spotlight as a luxury dyestuff. For example, the least expensive kermes-dyed scarlet in the wardrobe of the English king Henry VI (r.1422–1471) cost as much as a 15th-century master mason earned in two years and nine months. It was the best, brightest red dye around and was combined with other dyes to create a wide spectrum of colors. Kermes was often layered over woad blues: on pale blue cloth a kermes overdye will give you a jammy mulberry purple, and over a darker blue you'll get a deep eggplant. Layered over navy fabrics, kermes was used to make luxurious blacks.

Most famously, dyers used kermes to make scarlets. Understood now as the hyper-saturated red of vintage sports cars and classic lipstick, some historians argue that scarlet originally referred to a type of fine, woolen cloth of any color. Over the centuries it became associated with kermes (an expensive dye used on luxurious fabrics), and eventually came to mean the color of the dye itself.

The process of kermes dye extraction is similar to its genetic cousin, cochineal, though the life of the female kermes insect sounds even less prodigious than that of its immobile relative. As a young nymph, she chooses one branch of a tree (likely the kermes oak) to settle on, and feeds on its sap. It's here that she develops into her adult form, a process that includes losing her legs and growing a protective shell. After she mates she can lay as many as 6,500 eggs, all of which are contained inside her perfectly round, pea-sized body. After she lays these eggs she dies. Her decaying body protects the eggs until they are ready to hatch, and the life cycle starts all over again.

Once female kermes have laid their eggs, their bodies have the highest proportion of kermesic acid, the primary colorant in the dye, in their lives. It's at this stage, in May and June, that the insects are harvested—living or dead. And since kermes can't be farmed, historically, natural populations in wooded areas were carefully managed. This husbandry included protecting the valuable dyestuff from theft. In the late 15th century, the local authorities of Almansa, a region in southeast Spain, hired mounted guards each spring to watch over the insects as they reached maturity. The guards would stop anyone trying to enter the forest until the *rompimiento de la grana*, or kermes harvest, had officially begun.

The harvest would start at dawn each morning, when women and children would walk into the forest in search of kermes oaks. Once found, the bugs were plucked by hand. According to one 18th-century source, the women would grow their fingernails long to make harvesting kermes easier.

Once the kermes are picked, the processing method is almost identical to that of cochineal. Kermesic acid is an anthraquinone, like the red colorants in cochineal and madder, and behaves in a similar way. The kermes insects are boiled or steamed to prevent the eggs hatching, and then dried in the sun, ground into powder, and used as a dye.

When kermes are ready to be harvested they look like bulbous dust-covered berries, and if you're not looking too closely, a dried kermes could be confused for a shriveled chickpea. Whether fresh or dried, kermes' resemblance to various foodstuffs has caused a lot of confusion about the dye's origin (so have the "seeds" inside it—which are really hundreds of tiny eggs). Pliny the Elder refers to the kermes insect as "red kernels" and "berries." In Italian medieval and early modern dye recipes they're called *grana*, meaning "kernels" or "seeds." For one ancient Latin writer this seems to have been a call to culinary experimentation: "when chewed, these grains have a somewhat bitterish taste."

One 18th-century English dyers' notebook has instructions for "Cherries out of Grain." This may sound like a dessert recipe, but it's actually a method for dyeing wool red. Grain dyeing or "dyeing in grain" was shorthand for dyeing with kermes, and its reputation as a permanent, lightfast dye has made its way into our vocabulary in another way: think of an ingrained habit; something that's so deeply embedded it's hard to change.

Kermes has a few other etymological legacies. The word *crimson* is a riff on *kirmiz*, the Arabic word for kermes. Like scarlet, crimson once referred to fabric dyed with kermes, but over time it became synonymous with the velvety red color instead. In medieval European writings, kermes is called *vermelium*, *vermilium*, or *vermeio*—from the Latin *vermiculus* for "little worm." Even though kermes isn't what we would now consider a worm, it's frequently referred to as one, in everything from the Old Testament to a 14th-century BCE cuneiform tablet, to the medieval Latin dye manuals mentioned above. *Vermeio* is tied to a modern color name, too: it's the root

↓ In *The Virgin and Child* (*The Madonna with the Iris*), Albrecht Dürer painted with kermes lake red pigment, a bright red color obtained from kermesic acid offering a translucence suited to producing delicate washes and luminous effects

word for the orangey-red pigment vermilion (which is not actually made of the insects—it's a powdered mineral called cinnabar). That kermes has endured as part of the world's languages, including English's crimson, scarlet, and vermillion, is testament to the popular dyestuff's legacy.

And indeed, the use of kermes as a dyestuff goes back at least six millennia. In 1916, archaeologists uncovered red fibers and a jar of dried kermes insects in a cave at Adaouste in southern France, dating from the late-Neolithic age between 5,500 and 6,500 years ago. But what makes kermes more remarkable is the extensive trade routes, which—in combination with the kermes-dyed fabrics frequently found in the tombs of royalty—speak to kermes as a status symbol. In 1978, archaeologists found a kermes-dyed scarlet cloak at the 2,500-year-old burial site of a Celtic prince near the town of Stuttgart, Germany, far from the Mediterranean regions where the insects flourished. Meanwhile the kermes-red dye "Tyrian pink" decorates the hem of a frilled skirt found in central Asia, sewn sometime between the first and third centuries BCE, and in Egypt, kermes shows up on fragments of funerary cloth dating from the Ptolemaic period (305–30 BCE).

Kermes scarlets were separated in status from plant-based reds produced by madder. In the 13th century, several Italian city states ruled that kermes was the only dye allowed in the production of their signature "vermilion reds"—scarlet wools produced by the best artisans on the continent. This division was still in place centuries later. When the English king Edward VI was crowned in 1547, his list of accounts clearly separates the red, madder-dyed wool provided to the lower ranks of his household from the scarlet wools procured for the members of higher rank.

While kermes's competitor, cochineal, is still used on a craft scale for dyeing and commercially as a food colorant and cosmetic, kermes use is now rare. Today, very few of the insects survive due to deforestation and other ecological damage. Recent forest fires in the Mediterranean have destroyed much of their habitat, and their populations are slow to regenerate. Kermes are increasingly hard to find and unlikely to be commercially cultivated, so it's best to leave the kermes on the trees.

To Dye a *Crimson* Color

Adapted from *A Profitable Book of Cleaning and Dyeing Recipes* (1580/1605) by T. Bouck va Wondre (translated from the Dutch edition in 1605)

Scrape some hard soap into a pot filled with "common" water. Put your silk in a linen or thin canvas bag, then add the whole thing to the soapy water. Boil "softly" for half an hour, stirring frequently. Remove from the soapy water, take the silk out of the bag and rinse it twice: first in salt water, then in fresh water.

For each pound of silk, dissolve a pound or more of alum in cold water. Plunge the silk in (no bag this time) and let it sit for eight hours. Remove, rinse in fresh water, and wring it out.

Fill a separate pot with four ounces of crimson (kermes), and boil it with enough water to cover your silk, plus the width of four fingers. If you wish to scale up, for each pound of crimson color add three ounces of finely powdered oak galls or half an ounce of arsenic, an addition which the author admits is "not very wholesome because of the fumes."

Add your silk, boil it for 15 minutes, wring it out, and dry it in shade "so it will be fair."

Lac

Kerria lacca

Kingdom. Metazoa

Order. Hemiptera

Superfamily. Coccoidea

Family. Kerriidae

Other name. Common lac

Primary colorants. Laccaic acids, kermesic acid

Colors. Reds

Fastness. Excellent

Type of dye. Mordant/adjective

Other lac producers.

Kerria chinsensis. Chinese lac

WE MAY CALL BEES BUSY, but lac insects are the real multitaskers of the bug world. Lac produces beautiful, cherry red dyes, a natural resin that's been used to make everything from gramophone disks to jewelry to furniture polish, and to top it all off, lac insects secrete a sugary-sweet honeydew liquid that ants love to snack on. Where these scale insects settle, ants follow almost immediately. This relationship confused people for centuries. In China, early evidence of lac dyeing comes from 320 CE; the writer Chang Po describes red silk dyed with lac as *yicishu*—"red cloth from ant gum."

Lac insects are the final members of the Coccoidae superfamily—the scale insects that include cochineal and kermes and produce some of the world's most treasured red dyes. Lac are apple-seed-sized bugs and the source of warm red dyes ranging from tangerine to cinnamon to plum, depending on how they are applied. There are 13 different species, and the name comes from the Sanskrit *laksha* and Hindu *lakh*, meaning "one hundred thousand," referring to the swarms of tiny bugs visible on the branches of the trees they inhabit as parasites.

Lac are found in India, Southern China, Thailand, Malaysia, Laos, and Vietnam, where they have been cultivated for thousands of years. Though the lac is less well known in the West than cochineal or kermes, it is a dye of principal historical importance: lac is venerated in the fourth-century BCE Sanskrit treatise *Ashtadhyayi*, by the Indian scholar Panini. It was the primary red insect dye in China until the introduction of cochineal in the 17th century, and lac has even been found on fragments of wool in the ruins of Palmyra (in modern Syria), a city destroyed by the Romans in 273 CE, indicating extensive ancient trade routes. Lac was the pre-eminent red insect dye in India, a country that arguably has the richest textile and dye traditions of any in the world. And while dyers in Europe and the Americas may be less familiar with it than cochineal or kermes, it has earned a place in this book because of its rich and dynamic history as a dye, and its unique by-product, shellac.

Today, lac insects are best known for excreting shellac—a hard, shiny resin. Shellac is a natural thermoplastic, which means it becomes flexible and moldable when heated, but is stiff and solid when kept at room temperature. These characteristics meant that it was once in high demand for making early gramophone disks, as well as buttons and jewelry, and though synthetic plastics have mostly replaced shellac, lac is still used as an ingredient in everything from furniture wax to hairspray.

To get the red dye from lac insects you harvest the raw shellac (called stick lac) and then process it. Like cochineal and kermes, the whole affair begins with an infestation; in areas where lac insects are cultivated, farmers will put the bugs onto the trees they want them to infest. Then, the insects swarm along the branches until they find a tender twig to attach themselves to and feed on the sap. Lac live in over 90 different kinds of trees, preferring gum-producing species like acacia and ficus. They also don't mind close quarters; an average of 23 insects will live on a single square centimeter of twig. Once they've landed, the bugs begin molting—shedding their old outer layer to allow for growth. Unlike snakes, which also shed their skin, and crabs, which drop their shells, when lac insects molt it's a bit more spectacular: they lose not just an outer layer but their eyes and legs as well.

After they've molted, the female insects begin secreting shellac. Unlike cochineal, which covers itself with a waxy grayish white web, lac covering is a hard, glossy resin; globs of red-brown envelop the females. When infestations are thick, the blobs blend together, and a branch can resemble a brick of old-fashion rock candy.

The blob-covered branches are what is called stick lac, and it's from these that lac dye is extracted. First, the branches are cut off and laid out to dry. Depending on the species of lac, the resin will either fall off the branch easily, or need to be scraped off as chunks. These chunks are called crude lac.

On a craft scale, the dye extraction is simple; the crude lac is crushed into small pieces and soaked in water. After a time, the solution turns an opaque maroon, and the gummy lac resin is strained out, leaving the thick, blood-like dye. On an industrial scale this process includes chemical solutions which dissolve and precipitate the colorants. Even with contemporary processing methods, shellac resin is difficult to separate out completely, and dyers over the centuries have complained about residual resin.

Despite dyers in India using lac as a dye from at least the Vedic period (1500–500 BCE), textile artifacts from this time are scarce. Instead, our information about the earliest known uses of lac insects (both as shellac and as a dye) date from texts like the *Atharvaveda*, a sacred Indian scripture from 1500 BCE, and from a chapter of a famous Sanskrit epic, the *Mahăbhărata*, written between 300 BCE and 300 CE. The story of the Lakshagriha, or House of Lacquer, is an elaborate revenge plot in which the antagonist Duryodhana builds a highly flammable palace made from shellac. He then invites his enemies to stay, setting the palace alight while they are inside.

Evidence of lac trade is similarly piecemeal, though we know its ancient trade routes span from India to as far as the Mediterranean. The earliest example of trade is a lac-painted Italian wine jug (called an oinochoe) from the third century BCE. The wool fragments from Palmyra, mentioned earlier, are an additional testament to lac trading routes.

By the 11th century, lac pigments were being used for manuscript illumination. The oldest surviving recipes for making lac pigment are from *Ibn Bàdìs*, an Arabic manuscript from *c.*1025, with instructions for a "red ruby" ink made with lac, and from the *Mappae Clavicula*, a medieval Latin manuscript dating from between the ninth and 12th centuries. To make red paint for "wood and walls," the authors of the *Mappae Clavicula* advise grinding the lac, mixing it with concentrated urine and alum, and boiling it until the color is right. Despite this evidence of earlier use, lac pigments didn't become an essential part of European painters' palettes until the 14th century.

From the 16th to the 19th centuries, Lac was a key dye in the Ottoman Empire. In Bursa, the capital of Ottoman silk production over this period, it was the dye of choice for opulent silk velvets and was the source of the red found along the borders and within the intricate floral patterns of fine carpets.

The demand for lac reds steeply declined after the invention of synthetic dyes in the late 19th century, and it is now only used by artisanal dyers in small-scale production. And while the invention of plastics similarly threatened the shellac industry, the global shellac market was valued at

$156.4 million in 2020, with production expanding as consumers demand a shift away from petroleum-based plastics.

Today, shellac is widely used in the food industry, where it's known as "confectioner's glaze" and lends a protective, glossy sheen to everything from apples to jellybeans. Similarly, shellac is used in the pharmaceutical industry to coat capsules and tablets so they can be swallowed easily. Finally, it's widely used in cosmetics like eyeliner, mascara, and hairspray, where it has a range of functions: shellac is a binding agent, hair fixer, skin softener, and viscosity adjuster. So today when stick lac is processed, the once-valued colorants are often rinsed away so that the valuable, waxy resin can be put to use.

↓ A worker pressing sheets of shellac for gramophone records, *c.*1920

To Make *Pliny's* Purple

From: *Natural History* by Pliny the Elder (77 CE) (translated with an introduction and notes by John F. Healy).

Head to the Mediterranean Sea. Wear shorts. Do not arrange any social activities, because you'll smell terrible.

Catch some mollusks called *Hexaplex trunculus, Bolinus brandaris,* and *Stramonita haemastoma*. Do this by hand or with a clever trap. Collect as many as you can, ideally 160,000.

The mollusks have a white vein that contains a small amount of liquid, which Pliny says "shines faintly with a deep rosy color." Remove the shells of the larger mollusks, crush the smaller, and remove the white veins. Add salt (one pint per 100 pounds of mollusk veins) and leave the mix to stew for three days.

Then, add seven gallons of water per 50 pounds of mollusk veins, and heat the vein and salt mix in a lead pot at a moderate temperature. While it's boiling, skim the surface occasionally, as the murex veins will begin to float to the top. After nine days, filter the cauldron. Add washed fleece to the pot to test the color and let it soak for five hours. If it comes out a blackish hue, once it is rinsed you'll likely have the most desired color in ancient Rome: a purple "exactly the color of clotted blood."

Murex

Bolinus brandaris

Kingdom. Animalia

Order. Neogastropoda

Superfamily. Muricoidea

Family. Muricidae

Other names. Purple dye murex, spiny murex

Primary colorant. 6,6′-Dibromindigotin

Colors. Purples

Fastness. Excellent

Type of dye. Direct/vat

Other dye-producing murex.

Hexaplex trunculus. Banded dye-murex

Stramonita haemastoma. Red-mouthed rock shell, blood mouth, Florida dog winkle

MOHAMED GHASSEN NOUIRA'S OBSESSION with shellfish nearly got him kicked out of his family home. The Tunis-based Nouira, whose day job is in market research, is one of a handful of people in the world still making purple dye from the glands of predatory sea snails. For the past 14 years he's been trying to reproduce the famous Tyrian purple, the most valuable dye in the ancient Mediterranean. And it stinks. Nouira's wife became so frustrated by the terrible smell that she threatened to divorce him. Luckily, his dad offered him space in his garden shed, so Nouira's wife's threat hasn't been put to the test.

Nouira got the idea to make the historic dye as he walked along the beach one day with his wife. He spotted a small whorled shell glimmering red-purple in the sunlight, and it reminded him of a high-school history lesson on the ancient Phoenicians, who used several species of carnivorous sea snails (types of murex) to make hues that ranged from bright, clear lilacs to warm shades of plum, to blackish purples the color of ripe figs. Nouira was generally disinterested in history, but something about the Phoenicians and their dye had stuck. History tells us that he's not the only one to have fallen under murex's purple spell.

Murex purples were so celebrated and sought after in the ancient world that they were dubbed "royal purples," a name that first shows up carved into 3,000-year-old clay tablets written in Linear B (the earliest form of Greek), found in Knossos, an ancient city on the island of Crete which is now an archaeological site. Colors made from murex are also called Tyrian purple, after the city of Tyre, the center of the dye's Mediterranean production. Royal purples were expensive and time-consuming to produce, in limited supply, and at times more valuable than gold. They also had unparalleled staying power. When Alexander the Great captured the city of Susa (now in Iran) in 331 BCE, he found a collection of purple garments and cloth hidden in the treasury. The fabrics were nearly 200 years old and as vibrant as if pulled from the dye vat that day. According to Nouira, the fact that murex purples actually strengthen over time is one of the reasons for its enduring popularity.

The first few years of Nouira's trials making his own murex purples were the toughest. First, he had to find enough sea snails to make the dye, which he did by fostering relationships with local fishermen. These days he has regular access to three different species of purple-producing sea snail. The spiny murex (*Bolinus brandaris*) and banded dye-murex (*Hexaplex trunculus*) are spiky; they snag easily in nets, so fishermen often pull them out of the water by accident. The blood mouth murex (*Stramonita haemastoma*) has a smooth shell and must be hand caught; for these, Nouira works with divers, though he is determined not to repeat the mistakes of the ancients—overfishing once drove murex to near-extinction in the Mediterranean.

When Nouira started looking into how he could make dye there was little practical advice available, and his friends and family were skeptical of his new, smelly hobby. He took his time experimenting, combining recipes from antiquated sources with practical trials—though his first experiment took a surprising turn. After collecting a bag of murex and crushing them up (as per an ancient recipe), nothing happened. Frustrated, Nouira put the crushed snails in the garbage. When he opened the lid later, the trash was glowing bright purple.

Just as indigo needs chemical coaxing to make a blue dye, purple doesn't exist in the actual mollusks when they are alive. After they die, the precursors —chemicals that have the potential to become dye—morph when exposed to oxygen. This is why Nouira's first experiment wasn't an immediate success; the precursors in the murex needed time and air to turn purple.

Things get even more complicated because not all murex species have the same precursors or even make the same colorants. Most murex make violet-red 6,6′-dibromoindigotin, a less catchy name for Tyrian purple, and this is the colorant used most frequently for dyeing with murex. But *Hexaplex trunculus*, for example, makes indigotin and indirubin—the same compounds that indigo plants produce, and the source of a famous biblical blue.

Over the years Nouira has mastered the process of making dye out of murex. To begin, he crushes the shells. Then, he tears out the murex's hypobranchial gland (called the flower or the bloom), which contains the fluid that will create the dye, and coats it with salt; on contact with air and sunlight the shimmering solution oxidizes into a shifting rainbow of yellow, green, blue, and, eventually, purple. At this stage, Nouira dries the gland on a glass sheet and repeats the process with more murex. Then, making the pigment from the glands takes more scraping, filtering, drying, and grinding. In a 12-hour day Nouira is able to make just a quarter gram of pigment—and it takes four times that amount to dye a single shirt sleeve.

Letting nothing go to waste, Nouira eats the snails, mixing them into pasta or salad, or his favorite: murex boiled with salt and garlic, then egg-washed, breaded and fried ("it's like popcorn", he says). The crushed-up shells are baked in a kiln, slaked with water and then mixed into lime (calcium carbonate), which can be used as a building material, paint base, fertilizer, or as part of the dyeing process.

The origin story of murex purple dyeing has become the stuff of myth. It's also not dissimilar to Nouira's own experience. One day the Phoenician god Melqart (other versions of this legend say it was actually the muscular Greek demi-god Hercules) was strolling along a beach with his dog. The dog ran ahead, snuffling shells that it found along the shore. Melqart called to his dog, and it ran towards him, displaying a newly purple-stained nose. Melqart thought the color was so beautiful that he wanted to make a tunic of the same hue for his lover, the nymph Tyros. He set about scavenging for the sea snails, and from these created the most vibrant dye the world had ever seen.

Tracking murex purple's real-world origins has proven challenging. The earliest evidence of its use is from about 4,000 years ago in Qatar, in the Persian Gulf. Piles of murex shells and the remains of dyebaths on the Greek isle of Crete are a close second—at about 200 years younger. In 1969, archaeologists found dusty mauve powders on the Greek islands of Santorini and Rhodes, and analysis confirmed these were murex purples, probably used as pigments for painting walls.

A bronze-age palace in Tell Mishrife, Syria, holds the oldest known samples of royal purple fabrics. In 2002, archaeologists discovered a tomb below the palace that had been sealed since the Hittites, coming from Anatolia (modern-day Turkey) sacked the city over 3,000 years ago. There is evidence of dye-making, including purple blotches on the floors and purple stains on the inside of pots, and small pieces of finely woven purple wool fabrics.

Murex purples were the ancient Mediterranean equivalent of designer handbags and luxury watches. And like its modern-day counterparts, this status symbol inspired many imitations. Plant dyes were layered to mimic Tyrian purple. They offered less brilliant or less stable tints than the real thing, but like knock-offs today, they were close enough to the real thing for those looking for a symbol of luxury.

The Romans were relative latecomers to the purple craze, but from the third century BCE they picked up the color with gusto. Julius Caesar (100–44 BCE) decreed his officers wear purple robes—an unpopular decision at the time, since many Romans still associated murex dyes with rulers in Asia Minor, who had been dubbed "purple tyrants." Despite the grumbling, Caesar was set on purple, and passed laws regulating who could wear the color. Unsurprisingly, the most luxurious hues were for him and him alone.

Caesar's hardline approach may have set the tone for future emperors. For instance, Ptolemy, king of Mauretania (1 BCE–40 CE) visited the Roman Emperor Caligula in 40 CE, and in order to make an entrance he chose to wear a fine purple cloak. But Caligula was not impressed, and in response had Ptolemy murdered.

Under Roman emperor Alexander Severus (222–235 CE) the production of purple was also controlled by the state. While previously mussel fishermen, or *muriléguli*, had had status as free men, under Severus the law was changed, forcing the *muriléguli* to join a heavily regulated corporation and deliver quotas of murex to state-sanctioned dye houses.

By the first century CE there was such a thirst for purple that author and naval commander Pliny the Elder, whose recipe for making Tyrolian purple survives, dubbed the craze for the color *purpurae insania*—purple mania. Despite this purported zeal, however, neither he nor other ancient writers seem to have written accurate instructions for actually producing the dye. One archaeologist traveled to the Aegean Sea to try Pliny's recipe for herself, and was disappointed by the drab gray-violets (and odious smell) that the dye pot produced.

But like any other color, purple has gone in and out of fashion. In the fifth century BCE the color had been popular in Greece as a symbol of wealth and status; after the Greek Persian wars (492–449 BCE), the Greeks began to see expensive clothes as unfit for their culture, associating purple cloth with Persian monarchs, who had started wearing purple for ceremonial dress in the ninth century BCE. This association waned over time, however, and a century later purple was trending in Greece once again.

Murex purples have been used far beyond the Mediterranean for centuries as well, though species and methods for dye-making vary. In southwestern Japan, archaeologists have uncovered purple silk fragments tied to shell bracelets and a bronze dagger from the first century CE. Along the Pacific coast of Central America, piles of shells for purple production date back to around 1800 BCE. In Peru, burial textiles from between 600 and 1200 CE contain purple mollusk dyes. Today, the residents of Pinotepa de Don Luis on Mexico's Oaxacan coast form one of the few communities that continue to make purple the traditional way, using a knobbly, whorled species they call *tucohoyi tixinda*, as they have done for centuries. Sea snail dye even makes an appearance in the Old Testament, in which blue *tekhelet* purple and red *argamon* purple, both made from murexes, were used to dye sacred textiles.

For those unwilling or unable to produce the real thing, the Stockholm papyrus, a Greco-Egyptian dyer's handbook from the third century CE, offers an array of murex purple copycat recipes. "Making Purple Brilliant" is achieved by cooking alkanet (a herb in the borage family) with purging weed and wild cucumber or hellebore. Another recipe describes how a "Fine Excellent Purple" can be made over four days with mulberry juice and unripe bunches of grapes. When it comes to "Cold Dyeing of Purple Which is Done in the True Way," the author warns, "keep this as a secret matter because the purple has an extremely beautiful luster" that is "beyond all description."

By the third and fourth centuries CE, shades of violet and mauve, aubergine, and plum had become colors for the masses, which became an issue for Roman royalty. The reigning emperor, Diocletian (and later, Constantine), tried to claim the color back by connecting the most expensive murex red-purples with imperial power. He classified colors like the dark scarlet-purple *oxyblatta*, and the violet-blues of *hyacinthina* and amethystina as *sacer murex*—sacred purples—even inventing a mystic ritual called the *adoratio purpurae*, the adoration of purple, which involved courtiers kneeling before him and kissing the hem of his purple robe. And, of course, wearing purple silk was forbidden to anyone outside Diocletian's clique. Putting his money where his mouth was, Diocletian had one provincial governor and his son tortured and executed for ordering a purple robe from the imperial workshops without his permission.

Murex dyeing remained an important industry until 1453 when Constantinople, then held by the Christian Byzantines, fell to the Turks, and the last stronghold of purple production was no more. Shortly after, Pope Paul II stopped using purple made from murex to dye his cardinals' robes. Instead he insisted on scarlets, made from kermes that could be found in Christendom. As an added bonus, dyeing with kermes required an alum mordant—and the papal states happened to control all the alum production in Europe.

↓ The spines of a murex snail (*Murex brandaris*), 1940–1941

FUNGI

Orchil
Crottle
Wolf Lichen
Mushrooms

Fungal dyes are rarer than plant dyes and less venerated than the reds and purples made from insects and shellfish, but they're just as fascinating. This section explores some of the dyes made from spiny, webby lichens, the increasingly popular practice of mushroom dyeing, and the potential that fungi hold for the future of color.

To begin, *Orchil*, a jammy purple known for being both beautiful and ephemeral, famously used in the ancient Mediterranean to imitate (and adulterate) the royal purple made from murex. Second is *Crottle*, a cinnamon brown dye from Scotland used to make one of the world's most famous fabrics with potent cultural significance and a (seemingly contradictory) ecological impact. Next is *Wolf Lichen*, a chartreuse yellow dye currently used by an indigenous group that was once declared extinct—the autonomous Sinixt, whose ancestral territory in what is now the Kootenay valley in British Columbia was split by the national boundaries of the United States and Canada.

Finally, there's *Mushrooms*, which groups together the many wonderful mushrooms that have been used for dyeing in recent history.

Orchil

Sea orchils. *Roccella tinctoria, Roccella canariensis, Roccella fucicormis, Rocella phycopsis* **Land orchils.** *Ochrolechia parella, Pertusaria dealbescens, Ochrolechia tartarea*

Kingdom. Fungi

Order. Opegraphales

Other names. Archil, orchilla, orseille, tournsole, horizello, orizello, tornexel, raspa and litmus

Primary colorant. Orcein

Colors. Purples

Fastness. Fair

Type of dye. Direct

IN APRIL 1334, FRANCISCO SERENI was working as an *orxeller* (orchil gatherer) on the outskirts of a small fishing village on the Spanish island of Mallorca. He scaled treacherously steep cliffs along the coastline, stripping rocky outcrops of lichen species known as orchil that produce bright purple dyes of the same name. One day while he was hard at work, he slipped and plummeted to his death. While we don't know much else about Sereni's life, we know that his tragic accident was not an unusual one; being an orxeller was a dangerous job.

Orxellers repelled down craggy rockfaces filling bags with lichens—the webby mixes of fungi, alga, and cyanobacteria that grow from rocks and trees—before climbing back up. A 16th-century history of the Azores, an archipelago in the mid-Atlantic, describes some orchil pickers dangling in baskets that hung 50 meters down a cliff face, while others were suspended by a single rope around their waists. On Santa Maria, one island in the archipelago, the Rochas dos Dependidos, the Cliff of the Fallen, was named in memoriam to the many orchil pickers who had perished there.

Even pretending to be an orxeller could be dangerous. During a 1354 succession dispute between the kingdoms of Aragon and Mallorca (both now in Spain), spies from Aragon were known to lurk along the coastline of Mallorca disguised as orchil pickers in hopes of overhearing valuable intel. Any spy caught impersonating an orxeller was put to death.

Like indigo (see page 46), orchil isn't a single species. Instead, it's the name for both the lichens that produce vivid purple dyes and the dyes themselves, which range from the clear purples of wisteria blossoms to dark red-purple raisins. Like indigo, orchil has been referred to by a spate of different names. In just one 16th-century source, *The Plictho*, it's given four different titles, *horizello*, *orizello*, *tornexel*, and *raspa* (worth knowing in case any intrepid readers of this book stumble upon a recipe for horizello purple in future). Orchil is the second most famous purple dye, and if that doesn't feel immediately impressive, remember that first place, murex (see page 136), was known as "royal purple" and was so revered that one Roman emperor murdered a guest for showing up in a murex-purple cloak without clearing it with him first.

Orchil was murex's middling, mass-produced equivalent; a budget-friendly option for the last two millennia or so. Orchil dyes are direct, which means they don't need a mordant, and processing the lichens is simple (at least compared with the saga of making murex). But while murex dyes are famously permanent, orchil dyes fade quickly to washed-out grays and browns. As a result, they've long been outclassed by murex despite their popularity and widespread use.

Lichens are two—and sometimes more—organisms in one: a fungus and something that photosynthesizes, usually algae but sometimes cyanobacteria. The fungus is the dominant organism in the relationship. Unable to photosynthesize (make food for itself the way plants do), the fungus latches onto something that can, like algae. In return, the algae get a stable, protective environment. Botanist and lichenologist Robert Lücking argues that the relationship is an agricultural one: fungi manage the algae the way humans would crops of potatoes or corn.

Both the fungus and the photosynthesizer are opportunistic organisms. Lichens cover about 8 percent of the earth's surface, which is more than the land area of Russia, Canada, and China combined. And they're happy to make themselves at home just about anywhere. Lichens jut out from bald rockfaces that are salt-sprayed by crashing ocean waves below, but are just as content to creep across aging tombstones. There are lichens that form springy carpets on verdant forest floors and others that look like spindly pieces of coral. Some are gelatinous, others dusty; some have gently folded, leaf-like lobes.

One trait that all orchil lichens share is that they aren't purple. Though they produce bright purple dyes, the lichens themselves are drab browns, silver grays, or sallow yellows. The most famous one, *Roccella tinctoria*, is tufty gray-green with tapered, hairlike branches. Canary orchil (*Roccella canariensis*) is named after the Canary Islands, where it grows in abundance, and resembles a bundle of russet-colored twigs. Then there's the pale gray, skeletal Lima weed (*Roccella fuciformis*), which sprouts up along Mediterranean coastlines and on Atlantic islands near the equator. There are more orchil-producing lichens too—listed together they sound like the line-up for a music festival: peppered moon, crab's eye, and rock tripe.

Like indigo (see page 46) and murex (see page 136), orchil lichens contain precursors—compounds that need to be chemically transformed before they

A

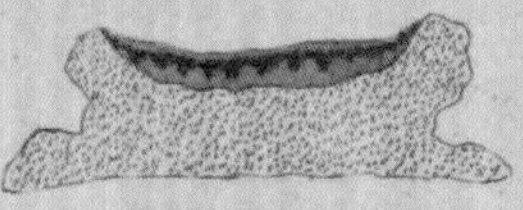

B

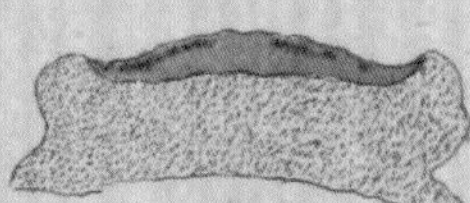

C

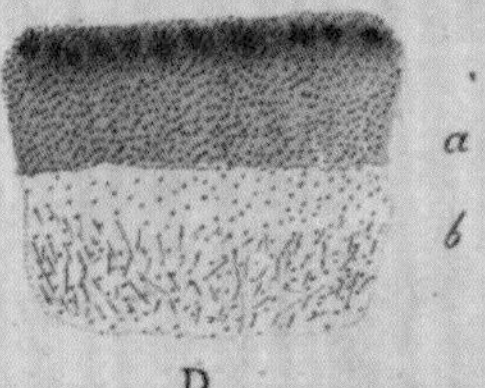

D

Kruskant laf.

Lichen ater Linn.

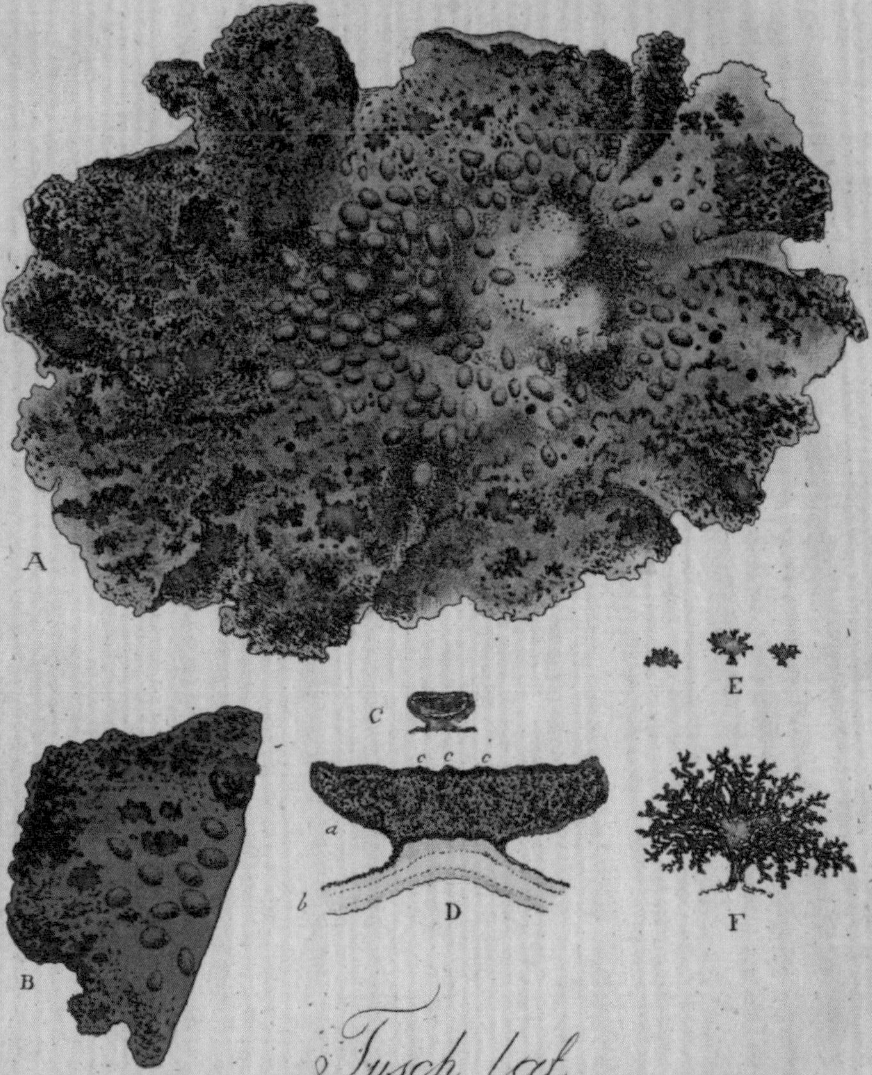

Tusch laf.

Lichen pustulatus Linn.

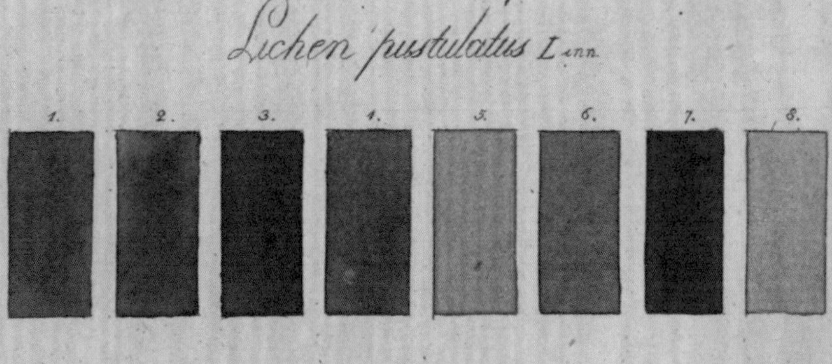

work as dyes. The colorant, orcein, is not present in the lichens. Instead, its precursor orcinol is extracted from the lichen and converted to orcein when exposed to ammonia and air. In practice, dyers prompted this reaction by crumbling the lichens into fine dust and steeping the powder in a foul-smelling mixture of water and ammonia, which was usually extracted from putrid urine and stank like weeks-old cat litter doused with rotten fish. In spite of the fetid ingredients, one 18th-century French dyer recorded that as orchil develops it begins to smell sweetly of violets.

As it develops, the orchil liquid changes color, becoming thick and opaque. It's a simple extraction but it's time-consuming. Leaching the precursor orcinol from the powdery lichen dust then converting it into orcein can take anywhere from a few weeks to a few months. The exact speed depends on the lichen used and the surrounding environment; the warmer it is, the quicker the chemical reactions will happen. At this stage, dyers have been known to add chalk or lime to thicken the mixture so that the purply sludge can be rolled into balls and stored indefinitely. In the Scottish Highlands, dyers wrapped these balls in dock leaves and peat-smoked the bundles to dry them, then stored them for future use.

As well as blending it with murex, historically dyers have used orchil to adjust other colors. In *The Plictho*, orchil is discussed as an overdye to turn faded blues into *morello*, dark blackberry purples. An earlier, 15th-century Venetian manual recommends orchil over a kermes dye to make the purplish red *paonazo* (peony) and to shift the brickish orange-reds of madder into imitation scarlets. Finally, as mentioned, dyers have used orchil on its own for millennia to achieve brilliant and affordable (though not exactly permanent) purples.

More than 4,000 years ago, Akkadians (in what is now central Iraq) made purple dye from what they referred to as a plant, called *puh* or *phukh*, which historians believe is probably an orchil lichen; the Akkadian *phukh* becomes *phykos*, a term that crops up as a purple dye in a range of later Greek and Latin texts. Theophrastus, a Greek scholar who lived in the fourth century BCE, recounts how *phykos* grows on the coastal rocks of islands like Crete and Candia and makes a dye more beautiful than shellfish purple (until it has a chance to fade). Writing a few hundred years later, in the first century CE, Pliny the Elder parrots Theophrastus's

← PREVIOUS SPREAD
Orchil illustrations, *Svenska lafvarnas Färghistoria* (The Dye History of Swedish Lichens), Johan Peter Westring, 1805–1809

take on orchil, almost to the letter. In the Stockholm papyrus, from the third century CE, orchil is used in recipes for making brilliant purple, genuine purple, bright red-purple, and the "Phoenician color"—a knock-off of the Phoenician's famous murex dyes. The volume of recipes for "imitation purple" hints at a flourishing industry of fake murex dyes. Orchil also turns up in recipes for woad, alkanet, and madder.

A few historical recipes combine orchil and murex purple, and for a long time historians assumed that dyers did this to keep costs down. But in 2012, Karen Diadick Casselman, an authority on lichen dyeing, and her fellow researcher Takako Terada experimented with these mixed purples, and discovered other benefits. Orchil and murex together gave the purest and most permanent dye—the orchil didn't fade, and, according to their reporting, the lichen neutralized murex's infamous stink.

After the third century CE orchil disappears from the historical record in Europe. Some scholars argue that this is because orchil dyeing stopped as a common practice. Their best guess is that like the practice of making shellfish purple, the art of orchil dyeing was lost after the Roman Empire collapsed in 476 CE and wasn't rediscovered until the Middle Ages. This theory credits a 13th-century Florentine trader with reintroducing orchil dyes to Italy after being awestruck by the deep plums and beet-purples that Middle Eastern dyers created with lichens while he was on a trip through the Levant, now the Eastern Mediterranean. The trader brought the technique to Florence, where it became wildly popular and made him so successful that he changed his surname to Ruccellai (after the Florentine designation for orchil). It's a widespread story, so popular that 18th-century botanist Carl Linnaeus named the *Roccella* lichen after the Ruccellai family.

Artifacts uncovered in the 1980s by archaeologists Penelope Walton Rogers and George Taylor have cast doubt on orchil's alleged disappearance across Europe. Walton Rogers and Taylor unearthed orchil-dyed silks from Viking and Anglo-Saxon settlements in London, York, and Dublin dating from the ninth and 10th centuries. At the time, these silks could have only come from one place, the Mediterranean, as it was the only region producing both silks and orchil dyes together. Even if the silks had been made in the Levant, they likely would have passed through Italy on the trade route to Britain, so the product and process couldn't have been as big a revelation as Ruccellai would have us believe. Walton Rogers also analyzed wool fragments from ninth- and 10th-century burial sites in Norway, Denmark, and Germany, and found that some of those wools, too, owed their faded hues to orchil. The wool scraps are orchil blended with indigo and madder, a combination that matches an orchil recipe from the Stockholm papyrus, dating from the third century CE, as well as later medieval instructions, which suggests there was at least some transference of knowledge between dyers over the millennia.

Demand for orchil spiked around 1500 CE. Once again it was being used as an underdye to cut costs for a more expensive color. Murex purples had faded from use but imported cochineal had spread its glorious scarlet across Europe. The orchil industry scaled up in response, establishing itself as an influential economic force on Atlantic islands like the Azores, Madeira, and the Canary Islands, where the lichen species flourished. Orchil was harvested annually, and picking the stuff off rocks wasn't an attractive job to most. As before, gatherers were required to hang precariously off the sides of cliffs. But in years when the harvest on the Canary Islands was poor for other crops, farmers and laborers looking to supplement their income would take the risk of harvesting lichens.

Production of orchil dyes in the Canaries and Azores dominated the industry until 1731, when an English sea captain found orchil on Cape Verde, a chain of 10 islands off the West coast of Africa. The Cape Verde orchil was plentiful—it was also bigger and better than the lichens from the Canaries. It's not known whether the bountiful lichens were a different species or if their generous size was due to an absence of annual orchil plundering.

In 1758, Scottish brothers George and Cuthbert Gordon patented a process for making dyes that ranged from pale lavender to inky blackberry with Scottish lichen varieties, hoping to compete with imports of foreign orchil. They called their dye Cudbear after their mother's maiden name, and despite some start-up troubles the venture was successful for a time, though the local origin of the dye soon became a hindrance as much as a marketing point. Cudbear manufacture stripped the land of the native purple-giving lichen species, and the brothers eventually resorted to importing foreign lichens for their production.

While orchil is no longer used to imitate more prestigious dyes like royal purple and scarlet, it's still used to make litmus paper, which reveals a substance's acidity or alkalinity by changing color. But the sluggish pace of lichen's growth poses an ethical dilemma when it comes to using them for dye. Modern dyers recommend looking for windfall lichens, specimens that have been scattered after stormy days, or ones that are being cleared for other reasons. So if your neighbor decides to scrape down the fungal algae that's built up on their patio, you may be in luck.

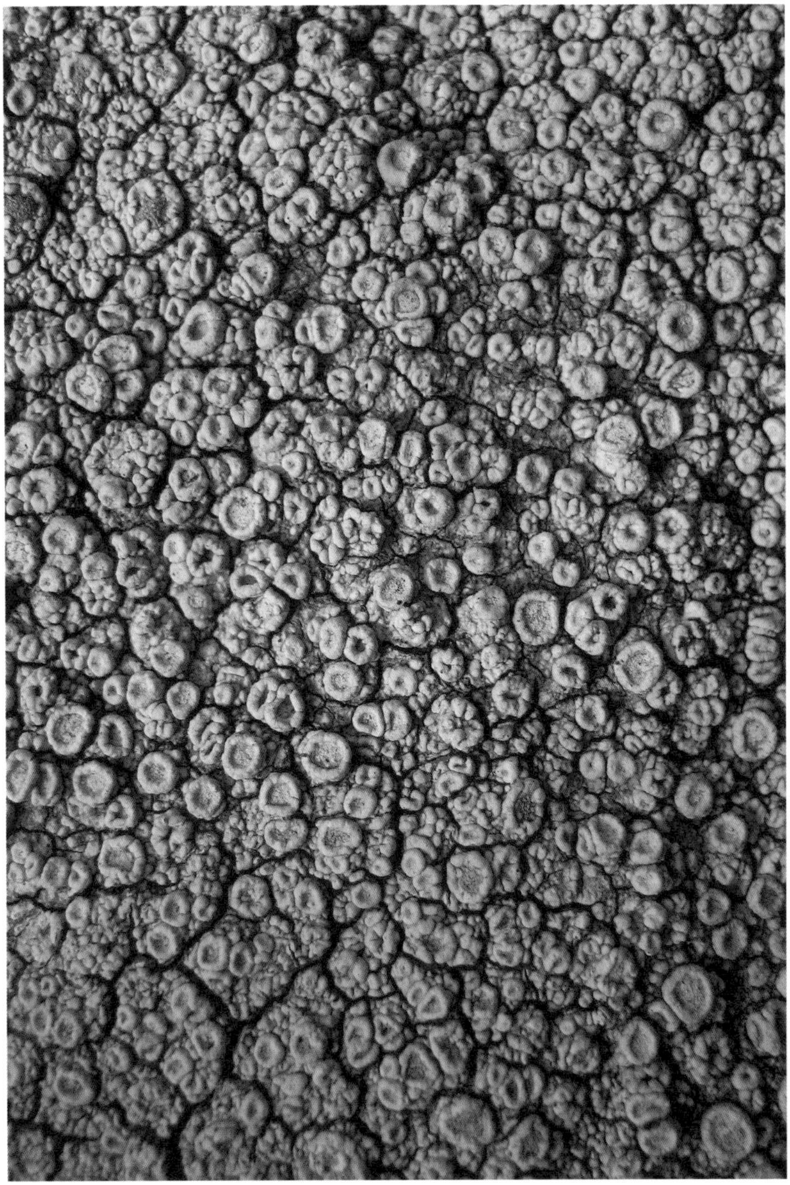

→ Orchil or
crab's eye lichen
(*Ochrolechia parella*)

To Make *Purple* from the Leyden Papyrus X

This recipe was originally called “A Second Recipe for Purple.” It’s one of many from the Leyden Papyrus X, and was adapted from the 1926 English translation by Earl Caley.

You’ll need a stone of Phrygia. But no one is sure what this is. Pliny says it’s a “porous mass like pumice”—modern scholars think it’s alum. According to the Leyden Papyrus, the stone of Phrygia should be roasted before you use it, and Pliny recommends saturating it with wine and then calcining it in a fire, heating it until it glows red, then “quenching” it with sweet wine. After repeating this process three times, break the stone of Phrygia into small pieces. (If this sounds arduous, quench yourself with sweet wine instead and use some alum you’ve bought from a store.)

Dissolve your fragments of Phrygian stone (or alum) in water. Bring it to a boil. Immerse the wool. Turn off the heat. Let the wool cool in the bath.

Throw “a mina of seaweed” into the vessel (a mina is the earliest known unit of weight, about 431 grams; the seaweed is likely orchil).

Bring the water to a boil. Add another mina of seaweed. Let it boil. Add the wool. Let it cool. Rinse with seawater for a bright, bold purple.

Crottle

Dark crottle. *Parmelia omphalodes*
Light crottle. *Parmelia saxatilis*

Kingdom. Fungi

Order. Lecanorales

Family. Parmeliaceae

Other names. Salted shield lichen, light crottle, human skull lichen

Primary colorants. Atranorin, salazinic acid, lobaric acid

Colors. Russets and browns

Fastness. Excellent

Type of dye. Direct

Other "crottles."

Xanthoria parietina, Lobaria pulmonaria

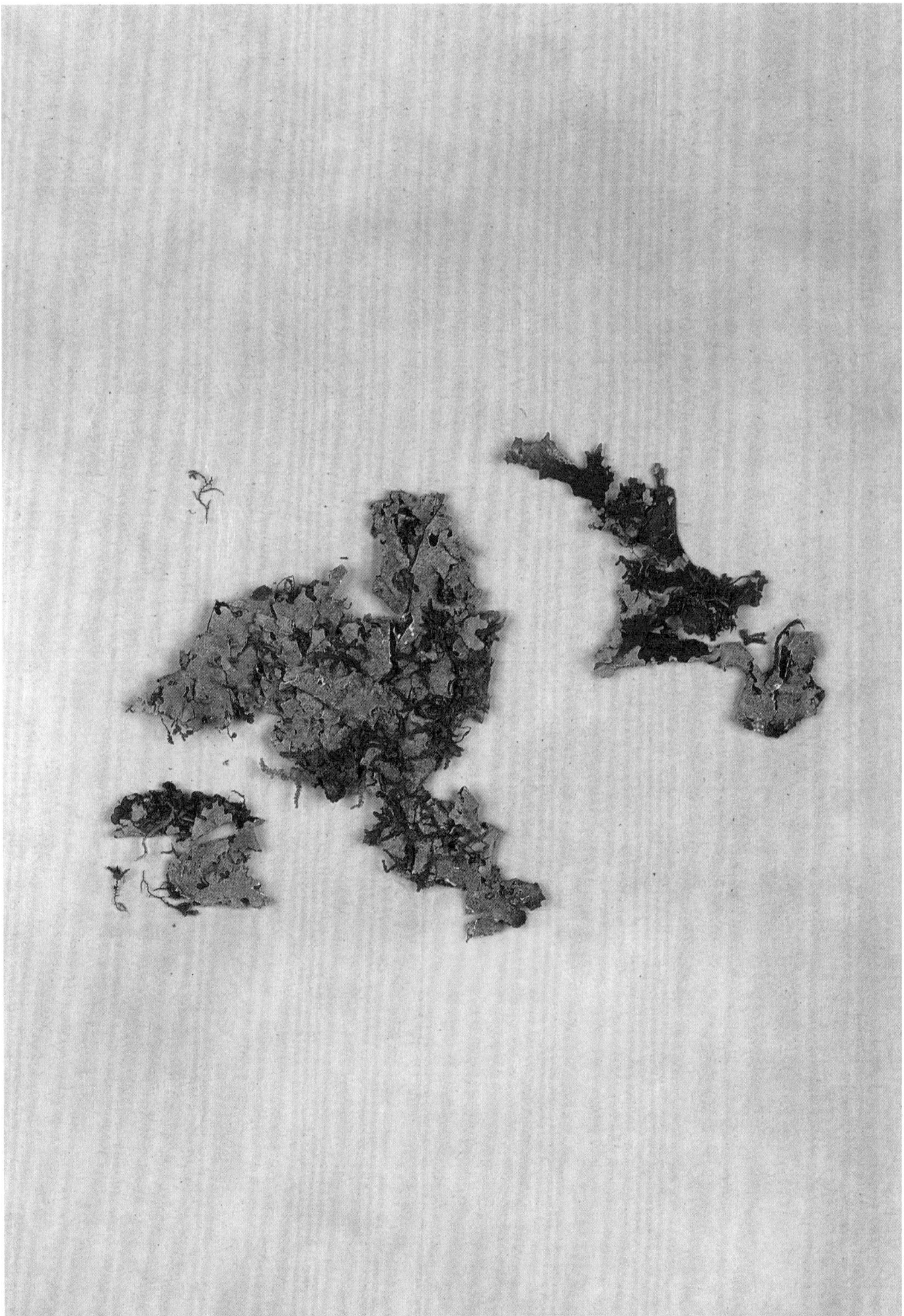

CROTTLE IS BEST KNOWN AS a dye for the thick, handwoven woollen fabric of the soft brown suits worn by stereotypical doddering history professors, and the greenish-grays of the English aristocracy's hunting gear: Harris Tweed. Harris Tweed is named after its place of origin, the Isle of Harris, a small island in the Hebridean archipelago perched off Scotland's Atlantic coast. To locals, the fabric is known as *clò mór* or *clò hearach,* which is Gaelic for *"big cloth,"* and it was once woven to shelter resident farmers from the windswept and harsh island climate. Harris Tweed first gained repute in the 19th century after Lady Dunmore inherited the isle of Harris after her husband's death. The wealthy widow found herself managing a 150,000-acre estate whose tenants had seen a decade's worth of hardship, from religious uprisings to the Highland potato famine. As part of a series of efforts to increase economic opportunities on the island, Lady Dunmore began marketing the locally produced tweeds to her society friends.

In the century and a half since, Harris Tweed has come to represent a certain type of British heritage. It's been worn by everyone from the sci-fi television stalwart Dr Who to pop icon Madonna, and co-opted by fashion houses like Vivienne Westwood, Alexander McQueen, and Chanel. The dense wool is the only fabric to be protected by its own Act of Parliament. In 1993, the newly formed Harris Tweed Authority ruled that if a fabric isn't made from pure virgin Hebridean wool, dyed, spun, handwoven, and finished in the Hebrides, then it can't be called Harris Tweed.

Originally, the caramel browns and tawny ochres characteristic of Harris Tweed came from a series of lichen species called crottle, or *crotal* in Gaelic. Crottle dyeing produces a gamut of warm browns from cinnamons to russets: "dark hazel" and "local tobacco," in the words of an 18th-century German lichenologist. While the exact lichen species used to dye can vary, crottle usually refers to two lichens separated by color: dark crottle (*Parmelia omphalodes*), a flat-laying lichen with thin red-gray lobes, and light crottle (*Parmelia saxatilis*), a paler silver-gray lichen that forms a delicately lobed crust on the boulders where it grows.

Light crottle is also known as salted shield lichen and skull lichen; according to folklore, if it was found growing on an old skull (especially one that belonged to an executed criminal) it would be an effective cure for epilepsy, could halt bleeding, and, if ground up and added to sweet wine, could treat a child's whooping cough. This lichen's supposed healing properties have a long history. In ancient Egypt it was mixed with mumia, a blackish resin that was scraped out of mummies to make a paste to smear on a weapon in order to heal a wound that had been caused by that weapon.

Though dark crottle lacks the—seemingly—remarkable medical properties of its counterpart, both species provide identical palettes of umber-brown dyes because the colorants in light and dark crottle are the same: atranorin, salazinic acid, and lobaric acid.

Crottle is unique in its geographic specificity. Most of the other dyes in this book were globally traded commodities at some point, but crottle is associated solely with the Hebrides. And while crottle is no longer used in the production of Harris Tweed, the cinnamon-hued dye has become synonymous with the thick tweed and its signature earthy smell that crottle has become a shorthand for a romanticized vision of rural Scottish life. According to lichen scholar Karen Diadick Casselman, modern crottle dyeing is usually a form of cultural re-enactment done to please tourists: "Crottle generates money. People will buy crottle-dyed cloth (and pay more for it) if they are told that's what it is."

Unfortunately, there aren't many surviving sources about crottle dyeing that predate the 20th century, and the ones that do exist offer few details. One late 19th-century account blandly describes 16 different dyes as "brown." From the information that is available, it seems likely that crottle dyeing was commonplace in Ireland and Scotland for centuries and that dyeing methods varied regionally. For example, in the Shetland Islands, dyers boiled crottle for two hours with stale urine until it reached the gloopy consistency of jelly, then added water and alum and simmered the cloth to be dyed. Across the sea in Ireland, dyers, spinners, and weavers worked together to make a similarly hefty wool fabric called Donegal Tweed.

Two memoirs by BBC broadcaster and producer Finlay J. Macdonald, who grew up the son of a weaver and crofter (tenant farmer) on the Isle

↑ Mrs McDonald dyeing in the open air to make Harris Tweed, Scotland, 1960

↓ Sheep being sheared, Outer Hebrides, Scotland, *c.*1920–1930

of Harris in the 1930s, offer the best-known narratives on crottle dyeing. *Crowdie and Cream* and *Crotal and White* are brimming with colorful tales from Macdonald's childhood on Harris, including his run-ins with crottle.

During the summers when Macdonald was a small boy, he and his mischievous best friend Gillespie would get roped into helping their mothers with the local lichen harvest. They'd head out in the morning armed with a sack and soup spoons cut diagonally to create an edge "as sharp as a pocket knife." They'd hike out onto the surrounding moors, bending low to scrape lichen off the rocks while getting readily distracted by the alluring tartness of wild blueberries and the intrigue of an abandoned bird's nest. Once they'd scraped together the first half-full bag of lichens, one of the women would call for the "half-sack break," a welcome rest marked by oatmeal scones and milk. The group only returned home once the bags were fit to burst with lichens.

According to Macdonald, the annual crottle harvest took place in early summer, after the spring shearing of the local sheep's thick, curly winter coats. Then, the crottle dyeing was done on a dry day in late summer, filling the warm village air with the heady smokiness of peat fires and the tangy scent of boiling lichens. To set up for the day, women in the village perched cavernous three-legged pots on stony hearths outside their homes. Then, they placed shells and stones in the bottom of the pots to provide a buffer from the heat and prevent the yarn from scorching. Unlike orchil (see page 148), crottle lichens don't require prolonged soaking in ammonia. The process is much simpler, not even requiring a mordant (although the odd recipe calls for one). The women would layer wet fleece and crottle in the pots like a lichen-and-wool lasagne, then fill the pots with water, light a fire underneath, and simmer the wool for a day, occasionally topping it up with water and a handful of common sorrel to "fasten the dye." In the days that followed, colorful fleeces and yarns were draped over every stone dyke and fence in the village.

The growing season on the Isle of Harris is short and lichens grow at a snail's pace, so by the time Macdonald was helping with the harvest in the 1930s, the rocks near his house had been scraped clean of the flat, crusty crottle that was so prized for dyeing. To avoid a long journey across the moors to gather the lichens, he proposed to his mother that he and Gillespie take a quick trip to the local graveyard to scrape some crottle off the sides of the tombstones—a suggestion that got him "howled down for sacrilege."

Macdonald's observation about dwindling stores was echoed by the larger community. To preserve what little remained of lichens growing on the local landscape, crottle dyes were rarely used after the Second World War. Nowadays, the soft, nutmeg browns of some of the most famous Harris Tweeds are made from synthetic dyes instead, while the crottle is left to slowly regrow.

↓ Dyed wool being lifted out of a dye pot and lowered into the machine that will dry the wool, Outer Hebrides, Scotland, 1970s

Wolf Lichen

Letharia vulpina

Kingdom. Fungi

Order. Lecanorales

Family. Parmeliaceae

Primary colorant. Vulpinic acid

Colors. Yellows

Fastness. Excellent

Type of dye. Direct

THE COLUMBIA RIVER IS THE LARGEST RIVER in North America that flows into the Pacific Ocean. It cuts a sinuous divide between mountain ranges as it winds from its headwaters in British Columbia down through Washington State and Oregon. The river's plateau—the terrain formed by millions of years of flowing water and geological tumult—is called the Columbia Basin. It's a proportionately large area (a little bigger than the size of France) made up of abundant forests and fertile valleys that extend across the Canada–US border. In 2017, dyer and artist Seathra Bell received a grant from the Columbia Kootenay Cultural Alliance to research the traditional dyes of the indigenous people who settled the Columbia Basin, where she grew up and lives today.

Bell worked with mother and daughter Marilyn James and Taress Alexis, two knowledge keepers from the Sinixt people, an indigenous group whose traditional territory was sliced in two when British Columbia became part of Canada in 1871 without any formal treaties with the Sinixt. Though around 80 percent of their territory was in Canada, most Sinixt were pushed south and those who remained were increasingly marginalized. Their religious practices were banned, as were festivals and dances, and children were taken from their families and forced to attend residential schools—the government-sanctioned Christian schools that aimed to convert indigenous youth, and which were notorious for their abusive and violent practices. In 1956 the Canadian government declared the Sinixt extinct (though many were alive south of the border), and their small reserve was handed over to the province of British Columbia.

James is a matriarch in her seventies who has been a Sinixt activist and advocate for decades. She worked with Bell to identify plants and fungi that her elders collected for dyeing when she was a young girl. Among them were the roots of the Oregon grape, an evergreen shrub that yields a greenish-yellow dye, alder cones for soft browns, common yarrow for tawny, blushing golds, and wolf lichen—the subject of this chapter—for dyes that range from sherbet lemon yellows to golds the color of ripe mango flesh.

The fluorescent, yellow-green Wolf lichen has tendril-like branches that grow to about 15 centimeters in length and resemble the inner networks of a human lung. It clings to the bark of ponderosa pines and other conifers high in the mountains of Europe and North America, making the trees look like they've got patchy coats of yellow fur.

The name wolf lichen is a nod to the spindly species' use as a poison for wolves and foxes that have strayed too close to human settlements. The Sámi, a group indigenous to northern Scandinavia, dried and powdered the lichens, then mixed them with crushed glass and reindeer meat to lure wolves into eating the deadly snack. According to James, the Sinixt used the luminous green lichen in an almost identical way. Vulpinic acid, the primary colorant in wolf lichen dyes, is the compound responsible for its toxicity, too, and is poisonous to humans as well as wolves.

Today, wolf lichen is important because it offers insight into a nearly lost material culture (the physical outputs of a society) and cultural practices in the Pacific Northwest. Its history is illustrative of what has happened to a lot of lesser-known dyes in areas that were colonized by Europeans over the last 500 years.

Some dyes, like cochineal (see page 108), were seen as valuable export commodities after their regions of origin were colonized, and the histories of such dyes have been well documented. Other dyes, like wolf lichen, were never produced or traded at scale, so their properties, histories, and uses are less widely documented. Many of the traditions of the Sinixt and other indigenous groups have been passed down primarily through spoken stories, not written ones, and as their populations were decimated (first by exposure to European diseases like smallpox, then by massacres and systematic destruction), this knowledge was diminished or lost. For information about dyes like wolf lichen we instead look to community elders like James, and to the material culture itself. For example, James has two intricately woven Sinixt baskets, brightly colored despite their age—300 and 500 years old, respectively. HPLC analysis (see page 110) has shown that the vibrant yellow patterns they contain have been dyed with wolf lichen.

Dyeing with wolf lichen is simple. It's a direct dye so doesn't require a mordant. Like crottle (see page 160), the dye can be extracted by boiling the whole lichen in water, which Bell says will fill the air with a delicious smell that is at once earthy and spicy. According to Alaska-based dyer and weaver Lily Hope (more on her shortly), wolf lichen yields its colorants faster if it's boiled with urine—though the smell is comparatively unpleasant. In either case, the dye liquid will turn an almost neon chartreuse thanks to the vulpinic acid. At this point, the fiber is added to the pot and gently heated, rendering shades ranging from pale lime to bright lemon depending on the concentration of lichen used and the season it was picked.

Lily Hope's heritage is Tlingit, an indigenous group whose traditional territory is now called Southeastern Alaska and northern British Columbia, and who are responsible for the wolf lichen's most recognizable use. *Naaxin*, which translates roughly as "fringe about the body," are Tinglit-woven ceremonial robes that are more widely known as Chilkat dancing blankets. Classic designs are centered around a crest animal or creature that would have been linked to the original wearer's clan identity, and stories are woven into the graceful curves and complicated geometric motifs that cover every inch of each blanket's surface. A single blanket can take a skilled weaver years of consistent work to finish.

The traditional dyestuffs used for the blankets include western hemlock, a type of spruce tree that produces reddish browns and blacks, copper oxide for sea-foam greens, and wolf lichen, alongside other local plants for yellows. Wolf lichen doesn't grow that far north, but it can be dried and powdered so is easily transportable and was traded to the Tlingit through routes that extended 1,500 km to the south. Unlike other available yellow dyestuffs that are best used fresh and so are limited by season, dried wolf lichen makes bright yellow dyes any time of the year.

Hope learned to weave and dye from her mother, who used store-bought synthetic acid dyes for her blankets—a common practice from the 1940s onwards. A foundational 1990 book, *The Chilkat Dancing Blanket*, by Cheryl Samuel, even lists the specific dyes from CIBA (a German chemical company) that come closest in color to the original natural dyes. Over the years Hope has moved away from synthetics, experimenting with the historic dyes of her forebears, and she shares the results with her wide community of followers online. Hope says that using natural dyes is a way for her to connect to the past—though she draws the line at foraging for her own fiber. Traditionally, the warps (or vertical strands) of Chilkat blankets are made from strands of cedar bark spun with fluffy mountain goat hair, which, unlike sheep's wool, isn't annually shorn. Instead, mountain goats molt in early summer, and the remnants of their winter coats would be collected from where they lay. It's a labor-intensive process, so modern dyers (Hope included) use imported merino instead, focusing energy on the dye process itself.

Practitioners like Hope and Bell, as well as knowledge keepers like James and Alexis, are working to recover and retain traditional skills and materials that have fallen out of use. Sharing their findings online—in their writings, image posts, and video tutorials—means that, thankfully, dyes like wolf lichen won't be lost to the past.

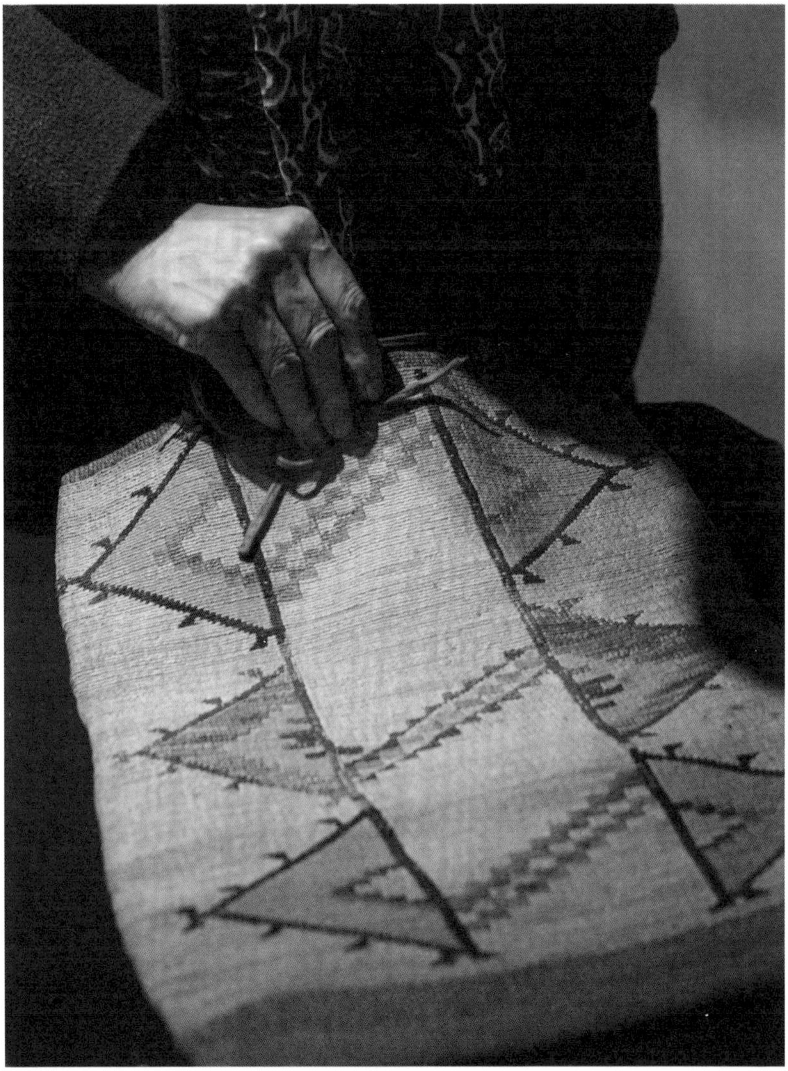

→ A 300-year-old corn husk basket colored by wolf lichen dye, producing shades from neon yellow to deep green

Mushrooms

Kingdom. Fungi

Dye-producing mushrooms.

Phaeolus schweinitzii. Dyer's polypore, dyer's mazegill, pine dye polypore

Phellodon niger. Black tooth fungus

Cortinarius sanguineus. Bloodred webcap

Pisolithus tinctorius. Dyer's puffball

Inonotus hispidus. Shaggy bracket

Mordanting mushrooms.

Laricifomes officinalis. Agarikon, quinine conk, enfant de pin, wabadou

Fomes fomentarius. Tinder bracket, hoof fungus

Polyporus mori. Mulberry polypore

A. CORTINARIUS ULIGINOSUS B. CORTINARIUS VENETUS C. CORTINARIUS ULIGINOSUS var. OBTUSUS
D. & D¹. CORTINARIUS MALICORIUS E. CORTINARIUS SEMISANGUINEUS F. CORTINARIUS CINNAMOMEUS
G. CORTINARIUS CINNAMOMEUS var. CROCEUS

ON A WINTER'S DAY IN 1974, Miriam C. Rice convinced a postman to hand-carry a shoebox from Mendocino, California, to the small town of Philo, 34 miles south. He delivered the parcel to the Philo postmistress, who telephoned Dorothy Beebee at El Ranch Navarro on the outskirts of town. Once summoned, Beebee hiked a mile and a half to the post office in the pouring rain, picked up the shoebox, and hiked back to the ranch, where she quickly dried off and unwrapped the parcel. Inside the box was a solitary eight-inch-tall shaggy mane mushroom (*Coprinus comatus*), which Beebee immediately began drawing—she had to. As soon as they're picked, shaggy mane mushrooms turn from pale bulbous eggs into inky black goo (this is called *deliquescing*—mushrooms do it to spread their spores). Beebee didn't have much time. She hastily made three pen-and-ink sketches, documenting the mushroom's disintegration.

Beebee is a retired scientific illustrator. In 1974 she was working on a new book about mushroom dyes, written by the pioneering dyer, artist, and postman-persuader Miriam C. Rice. Rice had gotten hooked on mushroom dyeing a few years earlier when her experiments with one locally foraged species, *Hypholoma fasciculare*, known as the sulfur tuft or clustered woodlover, turned wool a clear lemon yellow. She started voraciously collecting all the mushrooms she could get her hands on to keep up her dyeing experiments. In her words, "there were pots going all of the time all over the house." Her husband and children learned to be careful; what looked like an innocent pot of broth bubbling away on the stove might be a poisonous concoction of mushroom dye.

At first Rice didn't record her findings. She wasn't convinced her exploits would interest anyone, but a desire to replicate her early successful results and to understand the potential of each mushroom species led her to start taking meticulous notes. Rice's records were unprecedented: though dyers had long used mushrooms on an artisanal scale, there were no other known attempts to catalog species alongside their dyes. After years of research and experimentation, Rice produced and documented an entire rainbow of mushroom dyes, while her enthusiasm, courtesy of the book she made with Beebee, began to spread.

In 1985, after she had published a second book, she founded the International Mushroom Dye Institute in Mendocino, northern California.

Today, a new generation of mushroom dyers keep the institute going, and its biennial symposium has been hosted in countries as far afield as Australia, Estonia, and Spain. Past symposium sessions include Flurorescent *Phaeolus* Art, a workshop to make glow-in-the-dark pigments from a mushroom called dyer's polypore, Mushrooms Your Way, a class on cooking with foraged fungi, and Likeable Lichens, a deep-dive into dye lichens with well-known naturalist Dorothy Smullen.

These seemingly light-hearted sessions point to something of deeper importance. From psychedelics to stir-frys, humans have used mushrooms for everything from food and medicine to clothing and building materials for millennia. Mushrooms are fungi, and unlike plants they don't contain chlorophyll (the green substance that allows plants to make energy from light), so aren't able to feed themselves. Instead, they get nutrients from their surroundings, siphoning energy by breaking down dead matter, or from living animals, plants, and other fungi. We're most familiar with the fruiting bodies of mushrooms, which are the stalks and caps that we might add to an omlet or pasta, but there's plenty more going on beneath the surface. Fungi create a vast web of interconnected filaments called mycelium, which extend far below the soil and absorb water, pick up nutrients, and form a communication network with other plants that facilitates the distribution of nutrients and sugars throughout forests. This glorious network is referred to by mushroom enthusiasts as the "wood wide web."

In addition to an impressive list of other uses, mushrooms produce a whole variety of dyes. *Phellodon niger*, the black tooth fungus, so named because it looks like a rotting molar, dyes ocean blues and aquamarines, while the surprise web cap (*Cortinarius semisanguineus*), a slim, brown, gilled mushroom, dyes dusty peaches and corals. Dyer's polypore (*Phaeolus schweinitzii*), also called velvet top for its woolly textured surface, is one of the most common fungi dyes, giving bright amber golds on wool. The truffle-like dyer's puffball (*Pisolithus tinctorius*) looks like a rotten potato (other common names include dead man's foot, dog turd fungus, and dead horse fungus). Though the mushroom itself is undeniably ugly, the dyer's puffball produces wonderfully warm, rusty browns (it also has a characteristic smell that one forager compared to a "severely burnt tortilla").

Other mushrooms give everything from lemon yellows to mossy greens to purplish maroons, with an array of colorants responsible for this broad spectrum. Some of these colorants are the same ones that are at work in dye plants, others are unique to mushrooms. For example, the bloodred webcap is a spooky-looking, crimson-gilled mushroom with a slender stalk and bell-shaped cap that makes dyes ranging from mandarin orange to burgundy red. Its colorants are anthraquinones, which are in the same chemical family as alizarin, the primary colorant in madder. But some colorants, like hispidin, which is found in dyer's polypore and the shaggy bracket mushroom and dyes sunny yellows and marigold oranges, aren't widely found in plant dyes. Perhaps most intriguing is the potential for more mushroom colorants to be isolated and identified, pointing to an untapped rainbow world of potential.

There are comparatively few historical sources and less archaeological evidence of mushroom dyeing than are available for most other natural dyestuffs, but using mushrooms for dyeing dates to at least the 15th century in Europe, which we know because of the appearance of a few species in medieval Italian dye manuals. One of these is a mysterious ingredient included in countless scarlet dye recipes. In Venetian texts this substance is referred to as *opopo* or *popo*, in Genoese it's *oppopo*, while in Florentine it's *pococco*. It's not explained what the ingredient is, so it was probably so well known that the recipe writers didn't think it needed to be detailed —the way you wouldn't explain what sugar is in a recipe for cookies.

From the processes outlined in these medieval texts and the results they describe, our best guess is that *popo* was a mushroom that was used as a mordant. Like certain plants, some mushrooms work as mordants (more on plant mordants in *Metals That Bite*, see page 16), though the mechanisms aren't the same for all mushrooms—some contain acids like tartaric, oxalic, and malic acid, while some have high tannin contents and others bioaccumulate metals. Scholars think that the enigmatic *popos* are a type of polypore, which is a group of fungi known as shelf or bracket mushrooms. They're the ones that jut out from tree trunks like knobbly shelves.

Our best guesses for *popo* are the tinder bracket (*Fomes fomentarius*) a crusty, hoof-shaped polypore species found all over Europe, Asia, and North America, and the mulberry polypore (*Polyporus mori*), which is rarer.

→ Miriam C. Rice forages for mushrooms in the woods of Mendocino, California, 1990s

↓ Polypore fungus specimen,
Meise Botanic Garden

The mulberry polypore is a creamy yellow, kidney-shaped mushroom with veiny ridges, and, as the name suggests, it grows on mulberry trees, though occasionally it's found on willows and alders. It grows in Crimea, the Caucasus Mountains, Central Asia, and southern North America. Both the tinder bracket and mulberry polypore work as mordants, so they fit the brief.

The same medieval texts that call for *popo* mention another mushroom, *agaric*, which is used for mordanting and brightening wool. It's likely that agaric is agarikon (*Laricifomes officinalis*), also known as the quinine conk. In French, it's *enfant de pin*, pine tree's child, and in Ojibwe, *wabadou*, or white tinder fungus. Agarikon is a striped, puffy, and bulbous mushroom that can grow huge—imagine giant looming marshmallows suspended from tree trunks.

As well as being a mordant, agarikon offers potent antimicrobial and antibacterial properties; it's been used to successfully fight tuberculosis, staph infections and other ailments for millennia. In the first century CE, the Greek physician Dioscorides and our favorite Roman naturalist Pliny the Elder both refer to it as a medicine. The ancient Greeks named it *agarikon* because it came from Agaria, a region in Southern Russia inhabited by the Agaroi, a Scythian tribe renowned for their medicinal knowledge. Other species of mushroom are used as mordants, too. For example, the Bedouin of Kuwait and the Peul of Mali use fungi from different families in the same way as *popo* to mordant red dyes.

Mushrooms are increasingly being used at a craft scale for dyeing, but their biggest contribution to textiles might come in a completely different form. Every year the fashion industry uses around 93 billion cubic meters of water—enough to fill around 37 million Olympic swimming pools. The vast majority of this water is used in dyeing and finishing, and it's often released untreated into water supplies. Sometimes as much as 5–10 percent by volume of this wastewater is composed of excess dye, which is a problem because synthetic dyes are toxic at large scale and some are known to be carcinogenic over long periods of exposure.

This is where mushrooms come in. Treating water by passing it through a mycelium network is called mycofiltration, and early evidence from small-scale trials is encouraging. Using a mushroom's natural ability to suck up and concentrate contaminants could prove a cost-effective way to remove such contaminants from water. At present, the existing filtration methods we use require extensive planning and infrastructure, and can be expensive, while mycofiltration is cheap and straightforward.

At a basic level all you need is a burlap sack, some straw or woodchips, and saprophytic mycelium (fungi that feed on dead stuff). The mycelium grows around and through the sack, making a living filter, then the whole thing is placed in the water that needs cleaning, and the fungi-filter starts to do its job. It's possible that different mushroom species could be used to address a wide range of issues. For example, white-rot and brown-rot fungi have proven filtration abilities, black mold absorbs dyes from water, and other fungal species absorb copper. Further research and testing are needed, but so far mycofiltration shows a lot of promise.

Since Miriam Rice's pioneering efforts in the 1970s, mushroom dyeing has become a popular craft, and the world has also woken up to the endless possibilities of mushroom as medicines, dyes, filters, even vegan leather—all of which make an exciting departure from mushroom risotto and creamy tinned soup.

In the last few decades, online communities of avid lichen and mushroom dyers have flourished the world over, sharing knowledge, skills, and experience about their foraging, growing, and fungi dyeing. Rice's work continues to be expanded upon by contemporary dyers like Alissa Allen, who founded Mycopigments, an online platform dedicated to mushroom dyes, and Julie Beeler, who has created the *Mushroom Color Atlas*, an online directory of mushrooms for dyeing.

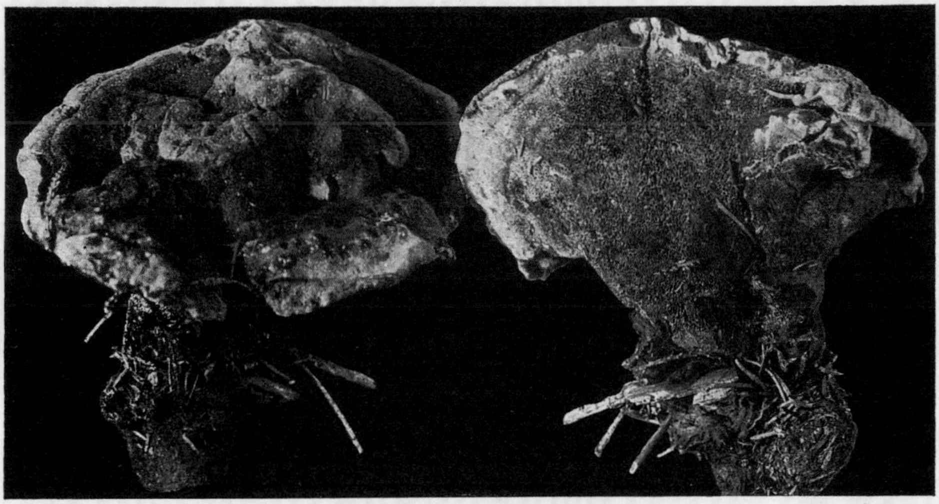

69. Phaeolus Schweinitzii (FR.) PAT.

Photo A. Pilát.

Čechoslovenia: Bohemia, Jevany, IX. - 1935, leg. V. Sak. $^1/_2$ orig.

↑ *Phaeolus schweinitzii* from *Atlas des champignons de l'Europe*, written by Karel Kavina and Alber Pilát, 1936–1942

→ Miriam C. Rice's original research into the extraction of pigment from mushrooms unlocked the full spectrum of colors, from delicate lavenders to deep reds to rich earth tones

FOSSIL FUELS

Mauveine
Magenta
Alizarin
Aniline Black
Indigo

In 1856, one teenager's accidental invention changed the face of the global dye industry. The discovery of *Mauveine* and the new synthetic dye industry that followed opened an organic chemistry can of worms,

with solvents, fertilizers, laxatives, adhesives, cosmetics, artificial sweeteners, and drugs like aspirin and morphine hitting the market soon after. In time, the dye companies grew into powerful pharmaceutical giants that, among other things, funded Hitler's rise to power. Some of these companies still exist today and continue to produce consumer products and dyes that make clothes colorful the world over.

Following mauveine is the story of *Magenta*, a vibrant pink dye that inspired an iconic designer and was a staple of Hollywood closets. Next is the story of *Aniline Black*, a fiery tale of legal battles lasting nearly a quarter of a century. *Alizarin*, a wine-red dye that is the primary colorant in madder, was the first synthetic dye to successfully copy a natural one. The last dye we'll explore in this section is synthetic *Indigo*, the invention of which brought the British Empire to its knees.

Mauveine

Primary colorant. Mauveine

Colors. Purples

IN JANUARY 1853 A FASHIONABLE SPANISH noblewoman named María Eugenia Ignacia Agustina de Palafox-Portocarrero de Guzmán y Kirkpatrick—better known as Eugénie de Montijo—married Napoleon III, France's ill-fated final monarch, becoming the last-ever empress of France. Empress Eugénie was the it girl of her age: doe-eyed, dark-haired, famously charming, and unfailingly fashionable. Her weakness for extravagant dresses led to a long-standing relationship with Charles Worth, a British dressmaker who, thanks in part to Eugénie's prodigious shopping habits, is now known as the father of haute couture. Her patronage similarly kickstarted the career of a young Parisian trunk maker, Louis Vuitton.

When the young empress stepped out in an ensemble, other women raced to copied it. So when she decided that mauve flattered her pale blue eyes, the Parisian streets were soon filled with women donning shades of lilac, violet, and heliotrope. It's likely Empress Eugénie even influenced her English counterpart and dear friend Queen Victoria, who wore a mauve velvet dress to her daughter's winter wedding in 1858, prompting newspapers like the *Illustrated London News* to report on the trend.

Mauve's popularity spread throughout Europe, becoming such a craze that British satirical magazine *Punch* deemed the fad "mauve measles," and described a sickness that was "spreading to so serious an extent that it is high time to consider by what means it may be checked." According to *Punch*, the grizzly symptoms started with a "measly rash of ribbons" and ended with people dressed in mauve from head to toe. Advice for managing an outbreak of mauve measles included "one good dose of ridicule."

The frothy lilac gowns worn by Empress Eugénie, Queen Victoria, and their well-heeled disciples were initially dyed with natural dyes like orchil, but these fashionable purples would soon be derived from a different source—a thick, oozing liquid called coal tar, which chemically transformed into a dazzlingly bright synthetic purple dye, mauveine.

Mauveine was the first mass-produced synthetic dye. It's an eye-wateringly vibrant purple that looks like a sticky pool of grape-flavored cough syrup, and when it hit the market in the late 1850s it caused a sensation thanks to its stability, cost, and the ongoing purple craze.

The base ingredient in mauveine was coal tar, an inky black goop that is the by-product of the coal-refining process called carbonization, which means it is purified by heating it in an environment without oxygen. Carbonization turns coal into more concentrated sooty black lumps that burn more cleanly, but it also creates a slurry of waste products—flammable gasses like methane and hydrogen, as well as ammonia, water, and coal tar.

In the early 19th century the global coal industry was rapidly expanding. Coal-powered steam trains chugged across distances in hours that would have taken weeks by horse; lamps fueled by coal gas lit up newly industrializing cities. The coal boom had, among other things, produced a glut of coal tar, and no one knew what to do with it. Burning coal tar produced thick clouds of noxious smoke, and burying it killed surrounding vegetation, so the most common way to get rid of tar was to dump it in open pits or local waterways. Scientists correspondingly spent decades experimenting with uses for the masses of sticky black sludge.

In 1841 a German chemist named August Wilhelm von Hofmann (who also shows up in the story of magenta, see page 199) was experimenting with coal tar and isolated aniline, an oily, colorless, fishy-smelling compound. Aniline had been discovered 15 years previously when chemists working with indigo plants had isolated the foul-smelling liquid—*anil* translates to indigo in Arabic, French, and Portuguese. But Hofmann's experiments were the first to isolate the substance from coal tar, and though he knew it had previously been made from indigo, he wasn't interested in pursuing aniline's colorful connection, he was more interested in what he considered to be its more noble uses, including in medicines. Over the next decade or so Hofmann isolated more compounds from coal tar, and in the process landed the coveted post of director at London's newly formed Royal College of Chemistry. Then, during the Easter break of 1856 he gave one of his bright young students some homework. Under Hofmann's direction, William Henry Perkin, aged 18, spent the holidays trying to make synthetic quinine out of aniline. Perkin accidentally discovered mauveine instead.

Quinine was the most effective known treatment for malaria (and is still used today). Among other things, obtaining adequate reserves of quinine offered a strategic advantage to the colonial powers, so the invention of a

↓ A fashion plate showing a woman in an aniline purple crinoline day dress, *c.*1860

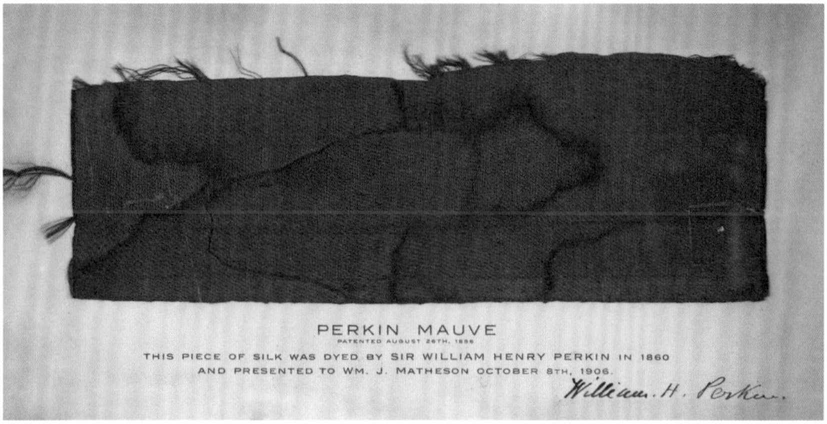
PERKIN MAUVE
THIS PIECE OF SILK WAS DYED BY SIR WILLIAM HENRY PERKIN IN 1860
AND PRESENTED TO WM. J. MATHESON OCTOBER 8TH, 1906.
William H. Perkin

↖ In 1856, while studying at the Royal College of Chemistry, William Henry Perkin discovered that aniline, derived from coal tar, could be mixed with alcohol, creating a black ferment that dyed fabrics a bright purple

↓ The Perkin factory at Greenford Green, Middlesex, *c.*1870

synthetic version promised its discoverer wealth and fame. Undaunted after failing to copy quinine's molecular structure from his makeshift attic lab in his parent's east London home, the teenage Perkin tried treating the murky, oily aniline solution with alcohol in an effort to puzzle out the nature of the reaction. But that didn't work either. Instead, the consequences were unexpectedly colorful; the solution turned a garish shade of violet.

The curious Perkin dipped a swatch of silk into the liquid, and when he removed it he saw that it had been stained lilac. In his own words, the solution was a "very stable compound dyeing silk a beautiful purple." Excited, Perkin shared the details of his discovery with his best friend and fellow chemistry student, Arthur Church, who encouraged Perkin to develop the dye into a product even though making aniline on a large scale was unprecedented and bound to be an expensive, difficult process. But buoyed by his friend's enthusiasm, Perkin set out to develop a saleable dye.

Over the next few weeks Perkin made more of the dye, moving from his attic to his back garden to scale up production. Seeking professional advice, he sent samples to John Pullar and Son of Perth, a leading Scottish dye firm. Robert Pullar, the firm's 28-year-old prodigal heir, responded with enthusiasm: "If your discovery does not make the goods too expensive it is decidedly one of the most valuable that has come out for a very long time." It was the start of an enduring friendship that helped Perkin get his purple to market. The two struck up a correspondence, and the younger man visited the Perthshire dye works, where Pullar introduced him to interested agents.

Perkin continued to expand his business, taking over his family's backroom and recruiting the help of his older brother, Thomas. His friend Church urged him to take out a patent, and Perkin likely convinced his father, a builder who had initially been skeptical of his son's scientific leanings, to pay for the costly patent.

But while his father might have backed Perkin's initial foray into business, his tutor Hofmann was less supportive. In late 1856 Perkin dropped out of the Royal College of Chemistry to focus on developing his invention. The esteemed college director, who had been Perkin's tutor since the boy was 15, argued that a purple dye might make Perkin some money, but such an endeavor fell short of the social and economic potential of something like quinine. Besides, Hoffman knew from experience that industrial chemistry could be a deadly game—the year before he had lost one of his star students, an aspiring entrepreneur who had died when one of his experiments caught fire. Despite his initial resistance, Hofmann came around over time and eventually got into the dye industry himself.

Within months Perkin had set up a factory on a six-and-a-half-acre site near Harrow, west London, and put his dye into production. He had initially called the dye Tyrian Purple in homage to the coveted ancient color (see page 138), but instead he decided to capitalize on the current fashion for mauve (French for the purple-hued mallow flower) and tagged *ine* on the end as a thoroughly modern chemistry reference.

Perkin's timing couldn't have been better. Pullar, his Scottish supporter, wrote to him: "I am glad to hear that a rage for your color has set in among that *all-powerful* class of the community—*The Ladies*. If they once take a mania for it and you can supply the demand, your fame and fortune are secure."

By the age of 21 Perkin had cemented himself as a successful businessman. Mauve, like all faddish hues, fell out of fashion in the following decades, becoming synonymous with a certain type of aging woman. As for Perkin, he would win and lose fortunes in the dye industry before retiring at 35 to a quiet life of research.

But long after mauve fell from fashion, Perkin was celebrated for kickstarting a modern industry. In 1906 he made a trip to New York to celebrate Mauveine's 50th anniversary at the city's leading dining hall, Delmonico's. *The New York Herald* headline read, "Coal Tar Wizard, Just Arrived in Country, Transmuted Liquid Dross to Gold," while 400 people (appropriately accessorized with mauve bowties and hair ribbons) gathered to dine on oysters, grouse, and clear green turtle soup, as they listened eagerly to the one-time wunderkind spin stories about his famous purple.

Magenta

Other names. Fuchsine, roseine, rosaniline, aniline red, rubine

Primary colorant. Fuchsine

Colors. Pinks to magentas (and can be used as a chemical base for many colors)

IN THE 1930S, THE AVANT-GARDE fashion designer Elsa Schiaparelli built an empire based on a single shade. Her signature color was "bright, impossible, impudent, becoming, life-giving ... pure and undiluted." She called it shocking pink.

Schiaparelli made dresses, hats, and accessories out of the vivid, punchy pink; she put it on perfume bottles and cosmetics packaging. Shocking pink is the famous fuchsia of Marilyn Monroe's strapless gown worn when she sang "Diamonds are a Girl's Best Friend," in *Gentlemen Prefer Blondes*—since copied by the likes of Madonna and Kylie Jenner. It's the color of the cursive curlicue logo of the world's best-selling doll, Barbie. In the 1930s the luminously bright pink was synonymous with Schiaparelli herself, and to this day cosmetics giant NARS makes a bestselling electric pink lipstick named in her honor, Schiap. Schiaparelli's shocking pink (and its legacy) likely wouldn't exist without synthetic dyes.

To make magenta naturally you need a careful blend of colorants. There's a bright pink swatch glued into one 18th-century British dyers' manual with a neatly scrawled recipe beside it that describes mordanting wool in alum and cream of tartar then dyeing with a blend of the tartar, cochineal, and madder. Even then, the color isn't quite Schiaparelli-worthy, and it would have been incredibly expensive. Before synthetic dyes were widely available, Schiaparelli's magenta obsession would have been shocking for a reason beyond its color: its price tag.

Regardless of its name, the popping purplish-pink magenta has long been divisive. Fashion legend Yves Saint Laurent called it "an aggressive, brawling ... pink" and the controversy hasn't always had to do with the color itself. Synthetic magenta was widely used throughout the 20th century to color everything from fine silks to hotdogs, but when it was first invented it was the subject of a heated patent debate, and its production even proved fatal (more on that to come).

Magenta was one of the first synthetic dyes to be developed after mauveine (see page 188), a product so popular that by the early 1860s a host of competitors had cropped up hoping to duplicate its success. On 8 April, 1859, French industrial chemist François-Emmanuel Verguin and his business partners, the Lyon-based dye firm Renard Frères (named for the owners, the Renard Brothers, who had a well-earned reputation as ruthless businessmen), took out a patent on a magenta dye process. In the months that followed, two English firms found a cheaper, faster way to produce the same dye and filed for the English patent within days of each other.

Like mauve, magenta is made from aniline, the oily, fishy-smelling liquid that is a coal tar derivative; the difference between the two dyes is the subsequent processes and chemicals that are added. Making magenta requires arsenic acid, or nitrobenzene—a process that was discovered later. The original arsenic acid method starts with aniline, which can be toxic if not handled properly, and also requires arsenic, a poison famous for exterminating rats (and cheating lovers). For manufacturers, part of magenta's appeal was its use as a base to make other colors. Mix it with more aniline and you get blue; with aldehyde, green; with alkyl halides, you get Hofmann's violets (named after inventor August Wilhelm von Hofmann—mauveine inventor William Henry Perkin's tutor, see page 191).

From 1860 to 1883, patents filed by all parties were the subject of heated lawsuits, with each patent holder fighting for control of magenta production. Verguin and the Renards claimed the French market, and a firm called Simpson, Maule, and Nicholson lay a claim to the English one. And while the English firm lost its bid, allowing a host of companies to produce magenta in the UK, Verguin and the Renards were able to establish a monopoly over magenta in France, where it was called fuchsine. (One theory is that the dye was named after the brothers—*Fuchs* is German for "fox," which is *renard* in French; others say it was an homage to the fuchsia, a teardrop-shaped pink flower.)

Alongside shocking pink, magenta dye has been called many things, from fuchsine to aniline red, rubine, roseine and rosaniline. But magenta is the moniker that stuck, originally given to the dye by Simpson, Maule, and Nicholson in honor of a famous 1859 battle near the Italian town of Magenta, which had been a decisive victory for the French over the Austrians. Though the connection may seem tenuous, Victorians often named new products after easily recognizable military figures and conquests (think Cardigan sweaters, named after a British Army general, and Wellington boots, so called for the military hero and one-time prime minister).

Over in Basel, Switzerland, Johann Jakob Müller-Pack was angling to get in on the action. Müller-Pack, an ambitious, broad-faced man with an impressive set of mutton-chop sideburns, had cut his teeth working for merchant-turned-Basel's biggest dye manufacturer J. G. Geigy. Müller-Pack rose through the ranks, and in 1861, at the age of 35, he bought part of the company from Geigy and began producing dyestuffs on his own.

Müller-Pack's primary venture was magenta, the hyper-saturated pink that would outpace Perkin's purple, and his story is synonymous with the greed, exploitation, and environmental issues that were characteristic of the synthetic dye industry in the decades that followed—and still exist to this day.

By setting up his factories just inside the Swiss borders with France and Germany, Müller-Pack managed to skirt those nations' patent laws and operate beyond the Renard brothers' control. He quickly expanded his interests with vigor. In 1862, Müller-Pack traveled to an international exhibition in London to showcase his dyes, where he won a medal for his "splendid collection of aniline colors" and rubbed shoulders with some of the biggest names in the industry. It's likely that during this trip he first met Heinrich Caro, then the leading inventor at the Manchester chemical firm Roberts, Dale, and Company, who sold Müller-Pack the rights to distribute a new color, aniline black (see page 214), an inky hue made from the waste of mauve processing.

Müller-Pack's company flourished. His operations were located in an ideal spot both geographically and commercially; proximity to the Rhine allowed for easy transport of raw materials and finished goods. Narrowly skirting the boundaries of France and Germany avoided patent legislation but encouraged neighborly trading. Moreover, the market, primed by mauveine, was hungry for new aniline colors—and magenta fitted the bill.

But this success came at a cost to Müller-Pack's employees and the residents of Basel. As can still be the case now, factory work at the time was characterized by long days, low wages, and little protection from accidents or site-related illness. Women staff often worked under the supervision of a male overseer or foreman and were frequently subject to sexual abuse and other forms of mistreatment. And the conditions

↓ Aniline dyeing at the Bayer Barmen Dye Works, Wuppertal-Elberfeld, Germany, 1900

at the Müller-Pack factories were poor—even by the low standards of the day. In addition, residents of Basel were growing increasingly concerned about the type of waste that was being produced by the new dye, and how Müller-Pack was disposing of it. According to regulation there should have been leakproof storage purpose-built for the factories' waste; instead, it was dumped into unlined pits that meant it could easily seep into the soil. Just one of Müller-Pack's factories consumed 200 kg of arsenic acid daily. Untreated wastewater from this process was released in the morning and afternoon, pouring into the Teich, a canal that fed into the Rhine. Arsenic, which famously has no smell or taste, has acute effects ranging from vomiting to muscle cramping to death. Even the dye that was produced at the factory could be contaminated.

While making fuchsine created residual arsenic, there was a simple way to keep it out of the water supply. When mixed with lime, the arsenic in the solution converts into an insoluble solid, so it can't enter water systems. The patent made this disposal process clear, but Müller-Pack simply didn't bother to use it.

It wasn't long before Müller-Pack's haphazard waste disposal caught the attention of local officials. Enter Friedrich Goppelsröder, the public chemist for the canton of Basel. He was the picture of a public health official: neat, bespectacled, with a long, well-tended beard and closely cropped hair. He was nothing if not meticulous—and it was his determined fastidiousness that eventually brought Müller-Pack to justice. Goppelsröder inspected the factory and made a series of recommendations to the Sanitary Commission. Industrial waste, he said, should be stored in leakproof lagoons, not in the unlined pits skirting the outer factory, where arsenic-ridden discharge could leach into cesspools. But despite an ardent report, Goppelsröder's advice went unheeded. His worry over the potential risks to public health continued to mount, and he kept lobbying the local government to take action.

A crisis was mounting as poisonous arsenic seeped daily into the ground. The residents started to take notice; at first there were reports of so-called "aniline gases" ruining laundry, and the situation quickly escalated. At the time, the primary source of public drinking water was the water table under Basel. In 1863, a railway worker had fallen seriously ill after consuming contaminated groundwater from one of the many wells dotted around the city.

Then, one spring day in 1864, the affluent Stampfer-Otto family sat down to tea at their stately home near the banks of the river Teich, close to Müller-Pack's factory. A violent illness overcame everyone who had imbibed the tea, including the family's maid and gardener.

Goppelsröder visited the Stampfer-Otto estate shortly after this incident, pumping out the well and collecting water samples, which analysis revealed contained residual aniline dyes and arsenic compounds. Alongside the strange smell and "yellowish" color, he found high proportions of arsenic in every sample. He used this evidence to push for a full investigation of the Müller-Pack factory and the water around it.

The Sanitary Commission dredged up sludge from the bed of the Teich canal and it contained so much colorant that it could dye silk. Goppelsröder tested over 60 soil samples from various depths below the dredged area, and the findings were staggering. The top layers of soil were visibly colored from dyes, and even at 23 feet deep there were strong aniline odors. At 26 feet, Goppelsröder and his team found astonishingly high concentrations of arsenic, while the rest of the inquiry painted a sad rainbow—blue and violet water, brown foam, thick brown-violet liquid—all tainted with aniline dye. The government's slapdash solution was to dig out the bed and cover it with cement, while the dug-up sludge from the Teich was to be thrown into the Rhine.

Goppelsröder's findings were enough to mount a lawsuit. After eight months of proceedings the court charged Müller-Pack with gross negligence and hit him with heavy fines. He was ordered to pay compensation to Basel residents affected by his toxic water and cover the cost of clean drinking water delivery. Only one of the seven affected people in the Stampfer-Otto household had made a full recovery; two of them were permanently disabled.

After this legal blow, Müller-Pack moved to Paris, taking his factory manager with him. This self-imposed exile proved a good move; he owned the rights to aniline black thanks to chemist Heinrich Caro, whose friendship still kept him in good stead. Müller-Pack profited handsomely

↗ Fuchsine production at the Bayer Uerdingen Dye Works, Krefeld, Germany, 1965

↓ Interior view of the fuchsine lab at the Bayer Uerdingen Dye Works, Krefeld, Germany, 1965

from aniline black, and successfully tried his hand at the silk garment trade. His disregard for regulation (and human life) doesn't seem to have greatly affected his reputation with some of the folks back home. Despite the wreckage left in his wake, twice he was declared a "free-thinking Grand Councillor of the Canton of Basel-Stadt."

The Müller-Pack case led to an 1866 regulation in Basel stipulating that dye factories "in regard to all their effluents, the neighbors and public must have no cause for complaints." Despite this government ban on arsenic dumping, the practice continued illegally on a large scale. The city was slower to react to similar concerns that arose over the production of fuchsine. It took 10 years after the intrepid Goppelsröder first lodged a complaint for the legislation to pass. Finally in 1872 the government made the manufacture of aniline red with arsenic acid illegal.

Unfortunately, the pollution of the Rhine didn't end with the aniline red ban. The river's water quality continued to deteriorate through to the mid-1970s, and in November 1986 a fire started in a chemical storage facility in Schweizerhalle, an industrial area past the outskirts of Basel. The warehouse belonged to the Swiss chemical company Sandoz, and the fire resulted in 20 tons of solvents, dyes, and pesticides flushing into the Rhine. The incident killed every fish in the river over a 400-km stretch.

Effluent from the textile industry continues to be one of the world's most pressing forms of aquatic pollution, though there is some hope for the treatment of the earth's waterways. In 2017, the Whanganui River on New Zealand's North Island became the first river in the world to receive personhood status. This means that the 290-km waterway has legal rights that can be enacted by appointed guardians—members of the Maori Whanganui tribes, who had petitioned the government for over a century and a half to protect the river.

Shortly after this ruling, the Uttarakhand High Court in India bestowed living person status on the Ganges and its main tributary, the Yamuna, though the ruling has since been overturned. While such efforts show a path towards change, they are the exception rather than the rule; the reality is that each year increasing numbers of aquatic environments are declared biologically dead.

Alizarin

Primary colorant. Alizarin

Colors. Reds

THE BAYER COMPANY, INC.

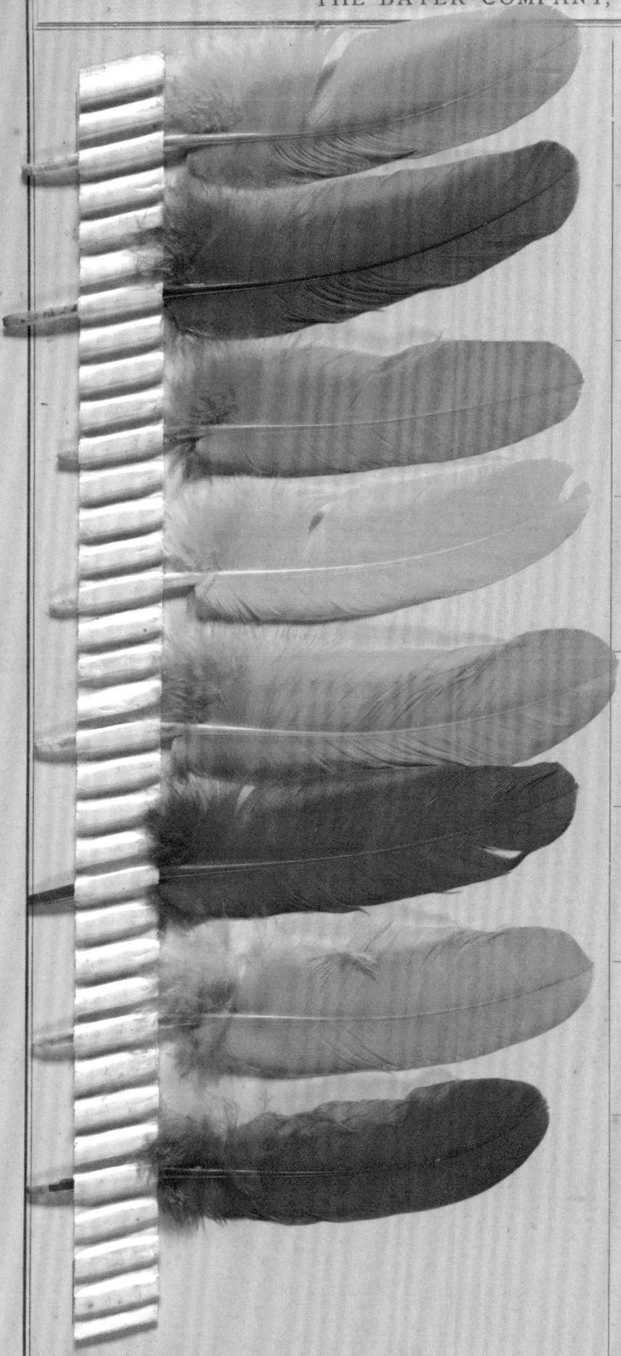

0,5% Azogrenadin S
0,5% Azo Crimson S
0,5% Azo Grenadine S

3 % Azogrenadin S
3 % Azo Crimson S
3 % Azo Grenadine S

0,5% Alizarinrubinol 5 G
0,5% Alizarine Rubinole 5 G
0,5% Alizarine Rubinol 5 G

3 % Alizarinrubinol 5 G
3 % Alizarine Rubinole 5 G
3 % Alizarine Rubinol 5 G

0,5% Carmoisin B
0,5% Carmoisine B
0,5% Cramoisine B

3 % Carmoisin B
3 % Carmoisine B
3 % Cramoisine B

0,5 % Azophloxin 2 G
0,5 % Azo Phloxine 2 G
0,5 % Azo Phloxine 2 G

3 % Azophloxin 2 G
3 % Azo Phloxine 2 G
3 % Azo Phloxine 2 G

IN 1826, FRENCH CHEMISTS Jean-Jacques Colin and Pierre Robiquet were experimenting with powdered madder roots when trial and error led them to astonishing results. Treating the dusty red madder powder—the world's oldest and most-used red dye (see page 74)—with sulfuric acid had isolated the principal colorant in the plant's knobbly roots. The duo had discovered the plant's chemical secret, used since time immemorial to make dyes ranging from warm, rosy pinks to maroons as deep as a full-bodied red wine. The pair gave the colorant the name *alizarine*, after *alizari*, the commercial word for madder roots, itself derived from the Arabic word for madder, (*al-'usara*, meaning juice). They later dropped the "e."

Colin and Robiquet's discovery was the first step in a series that led to synthetic alizarin—the first synthetic colorant to mimic a natural one. Mauveine and magenta were completely new substances; they could not be found in nature, and while their discovery was significant, making a synthetic version of an existing colorant—especially one as economically and culturally potent as madder—was a much bigger deal.

That they were able to take gloopy coal tar, a cheap industrial by-product, and with a few chemical processes transform it into a synthetic madder dye was nothing short of an industrial miracle. And, unlike natural madder, synthetic alizarin isn't an agricultural product—it's impervious to the scourges of droughts or floods or pests, and producible at a massive scale. It was the dye industry equivalent of turning lead into gold.

But we're getting ahead of ourselves. It would be another 43 years before synthetic alizarin hit the market, though the lead-up to its launch is quite the story.

While Colin and Robiquet were hard at work in their Paris lab, the scientific exploration of dyes was becoming increasingly lucrative. New machinery and advancements in chemistry were making consumer products cheaper and more readily available. Stuff that we now take for granted, like reliable bleach, chocolate milk powder, and strike-anywhere matches, were all cutting-edge scientific advances when they were introduced 200 years ago. And the dye industry was no different; coloring, printing, and other chemical processes were becoming faster, more efficient, and less expensive. The textile industry was on the lookout for the next big development, and big pay-outs awaited anyone whose innovation improved their bottom lines. Earlier in the century, one French industrial society even offered a 2,000-franc cash prize for the best chemical analysis of madder.

Luckily for Colin and Robiquet, a trend for red textiles went hand-in-hand with the drive for better industrial tech. Red chintzes—brightly colored, intricately block-printed cottons from India—were so wildly popular that governments in both France and England banned their import, (rightly) perceiving the elaborately patterned cloth as threats to their local industries. Though European manufacturers lacked the skills and technology to make chintzes of the same quality as Indian ones, they tried to keep up with demand by making cheap knock-offs of their own. Turkey red production had spread across Europe, and madder was booming (see page 80).

Colin and Robiquet called their turbo-charged madder dye *garancine*. In French, madder is *garance*, and they added the *ine* for scientific panache. Garancine was a chocolate-brown powder, odorless and tasteless, and, crucially, it was a more reliable dye than the powdered madder root alone. A French mercantile house bought the patent, and around 1839 factories began popping up in France, Britain, and Holland. Garancine hit the market, and its production quickly escalated.

At the same time, scientists were ramping up their research into colorants, though the decades between concentrating natural madder into garancine and the launch of synthetic alizarin were punctuated by scientific missteps. In 1850, chemists thought that they had worked out alizarin's chemical structure—the molecular code that tells you how a substance is put together.

The chemical structure is the scientific equivalent of an Ikea assembly manual; in theory, the instructions help you understand how something is assembled (though as anyone who has ever tried to assemble flatpack furniture knows, instructions are not necessarily a guarantee of success).

But the scientists got alizarin's structure wrong. They had linked it to naphthalene, another coal tar derivative with many common uses (in

↑ A partial view of the Bayer Elberfeld Dye Works which details the alizarin factory, Wuppertal-Elberfeld, Germany, 1887

← Dyeing in an alizarin laboratory, Bayer Leverkusen Dye Works, Germany, 1938

mothballs, for one, until we realized it was poisoning humans as well as moths), and it was almost 20 years before this error was corrected. In 1868, two German chemists, Carl Liebermann and Carl Graebe, proposed a new formula that led the pair to start experimenting with anthracene, another component of coal tar, because it had a similar carbon structure to alizarin, at least theoretically.

The two were in luck, and by the summer of the same year, Liebermann and Graebe had managed to make the first samples of synthetic alizarin—and it was eye-wateringly expensive. They'd used a chemical called bromine, which was far too pricey to be commercially viable, and the process they had devised was too complicated for any factory to follow. Still, their discovery proved that making alizarin from anthracene was possible, and the age of synthetic madder was edging ever closer.

A year later, in 1869, three different chemists successfully made synthetic alizarin using sulfuric acid instead of bromine: William Perkin, the creator of mauveine, Ferdinand Riese, working for Hoechst, and Carl Graebe, working with Heinrich Caro at BASF. Perkin and BASF filed patents within a day of each other and agreed to split the market to avoid a legal battle—Perkin would cover the British market; BASF would sell in mainland Europe.

Synthetic alizarin was an instant success. Dyers were accustomed to refined forms of natural alizarin, like garancine, and the synthetic version used the same process, making it an easy sell. Some even claimed that it might be better for the environment. One source joyfully proclaimed, "Thousands of acres of land in many different parts of the world will be relieved from the necessity of growing madder ... In this sense may the theoretical chemist be said ... to have increased the boundaries of the globe." The unbridled optimism about alizarin and other advances in chemistry persisted, despite the growing impacts of pollution from dyes (see *Magenta*, page 196). At the time, synthetic alizarin was alchemy made real.

In Britain, Perkin got lucky when the Franco-Prussian War caused supply chain and production disruption across Europe, making his company the sole supplier of synthetic alizarin globally. By 1873, the 35-year-old Perkin had become a rich man (again).

Due to the widespread availability of the cheaper, more reliable red dye, the price of natural madder plummeted. In 1865 a quintal (100 kg) of madder cost 200 francs; a decade later, it cost just 25 francs. One madder farmer, lamenting the loss of his livelihood, argued that madder offered more than alizarin—some colors, like warm cinnamon-chocolate browns, could only be made with the real thing because they needed the complex mix of colorants that could only be found in the plants.

And while we associate synthetics with industrial production, the new availability of synthetic dyes caused a boom in some small craft techniques. Turkish rug sales, for example, soared. Dyeing with synthetics was so easy that the spinners and weavers could do it themselves, without having to rely on the expertise of the old guild dyers, as they had done previously, which meant prices dropped and carpet sales skyrocketed.

Synthetic alizarin is still in use today as a staining agent for calcium in biological research, but not even this revolutionary discovery has been immune to the fast pace of innovation. In 1889 a German dye firm created para red, a bright, brilliant crimson that was cheaper to produce, and the sales of alizarin fell almost overnight.

→ Alizarin dye process at the Bayer Leverkusen Dye Works, Germany, 1961

Aniline Black

Colors. Black

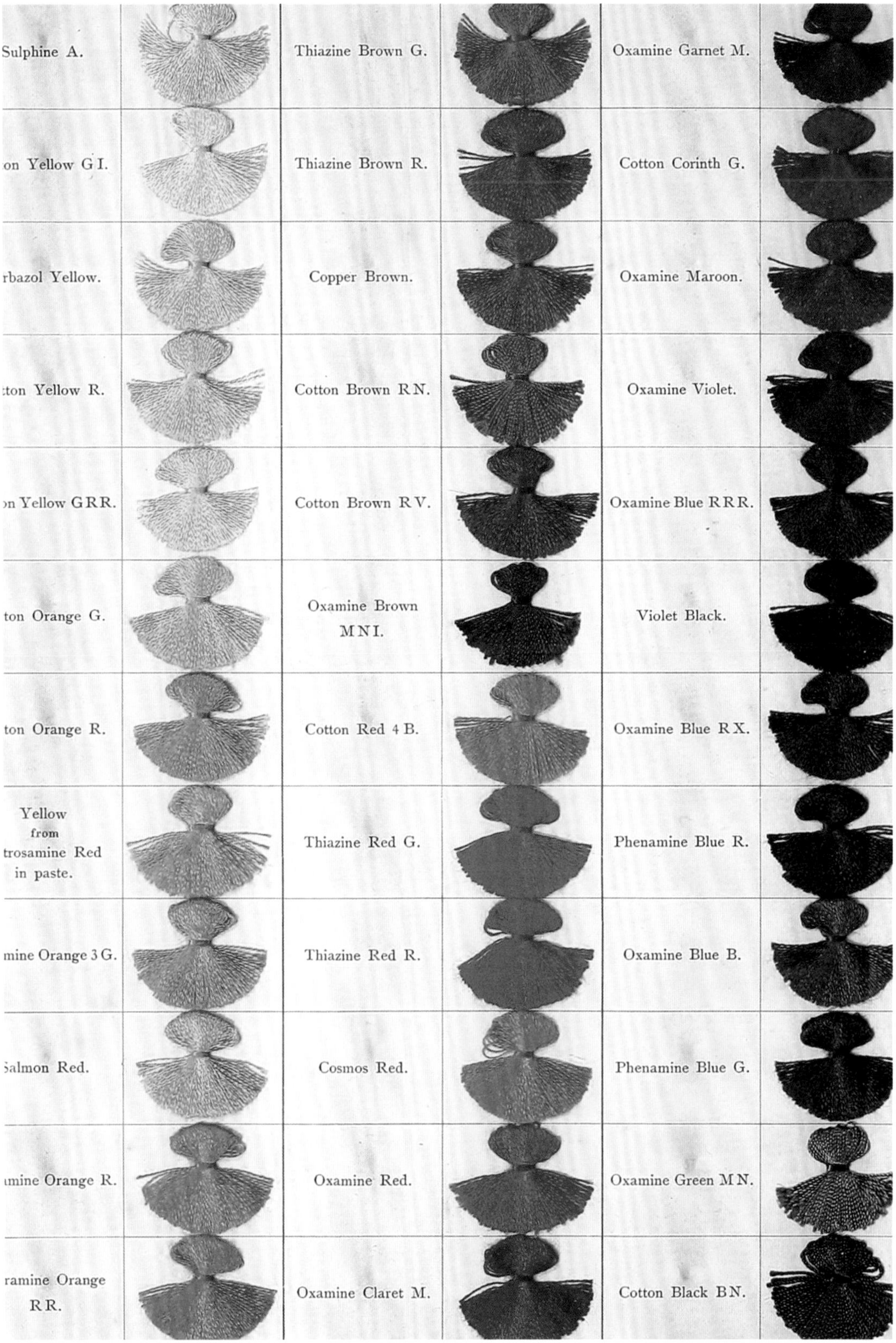
Sulphine A.
on Yellow G I.
rbazol Yellow.
tton Yellow R.
on Yellow G R R.
ton Orange G.
ton Orange R.
Yellow from trosamine Red in paste.
mine Orange 3 G.
Salmon Red.
mine Orange R.
ramine Orange R R.
Thiazine Brown G.
Thiazine Brown R.
Copper Brown.
Cotton Brown R N.
Cotton Brown R V.
Oxamine Brown M N I.
Cotton Red 4 B.
Thiazine Red G.
Thiazine Red R.
Cosmos Red.
Oxamine Red.
Oxamine Claret M.
Oxamine Garnet M.
Cotton Corinth G.
Oxamine Maroon.
Oxamine Violet.
Oxamine Blue R R R.
Violet Black.
Oxamine Blue R X.
Phenamine Blue R.
Oxamine Blue B.
Phenamine Blue G.
Oxamine Green M N.
Cotton Black B N.

ACCORDING TO THE FAMED Victorian novelist Charles Dickens, in 1860 the city of London wore a "grimy suit of mourning." The streets were dark and buildings were stained with soot; Britain's capital was a maze of narrow, smog-filled alleyways. At the time, coal powered almost everything. It warmed homes, lit streets, and fueled steam trains, while its by-products were being used to make household goods like soap, as well as a growing palette of dyes. The gowns of the fashionable set were dyed with mauveine and magenta, and a slew of new synthetic colors made from coal tar were soon to join the roster. But the success of this industrial product had cast a heavy shadow over the city. Thanks to growing numbers of factories and tens of thousands of domestic coal fires burning daily, the air was so soot-filled that the coats of sheep grazing in Regent's Park in central London were known to turn from fluffy white to dark gray in a matter of days.

The black lumps of coal were coloring the age in more ways than one. It covered the faces and lungs of miners who ventured underground, while the smoke blackened the buildings of industrial centers across the country. Coal was an industry on the upswing; in 1858, 172 million tons was produced worldwide—by 1905 this had jumped more than 500 percent, to 928 million tons.

Despite its proliferation and visible effects, chemists hadn't yet worked out how to get a good black dye from coal tar, though this was not from lack of trying. Black was a popular color in Europe at the time, having retained its long associations with sobriety and moral virtue. Priests wore black. So did judges. Black suits lent gravitas to a new class of businessmen—clerks, bankers, and accountants—hoping to garner respect. To top this off, the ever-influential Queen Victoria started mourning the death of her beloved Prince Albert in 1861, and for the 40 years of her reign after that she appeared exclusively in somber black gowns with inky-black lace and charcoal-colored velvet trims.

Despite the outpouring of resources spent trying to produce a reliable black dye from coal tar, aniline black was discovered by accident. It is a lesser-known color in the world of dyes, but when it was first discovered the commercial success of aniline black rivaled the synthetic versions of alizarin and indigo. It was also a paradoxical invention: synthetic dyes were a new high-tech industry, but the first version of aniline black only worked with woodblocks—an ancient method of printing.

Even though the scientific world was bursting with chemistry breakthroughs, it took decades to figure out the molecular structure of aniline black—no one actually knew what it was or how it worked. Chemists had figured out the molecular structure of other dyes, but aniline black was still being made by the traditional, empirical method. If you followed the recipe, you'd get aniline black. You changed the results by adding ingredients, watching what happened, and recording the findings. No one understood the chemical theory behind it, which fed a patent war that spanned decades and continents; it's difficult to defend a patent for something if you don't really know what it is.

In 1859, John Emanuel Lightfoot was working as a chemist for the Broad Oak Printworks in Lancashire, in the northwest of England. At the time, Broad Oak Printworks primarily used metal roller printers, which were ultra-modern, state-of-the-art technology. Instead of using traditional woodblocks—carved wooden stamps covered with a dye-paste and plonked individually onto fabric—the metal rollers could print meters of fabric in a smooth, continuous motion. Woodblock printing requires time and is the work of skilled artisans; roller printing machines can churn out meters upon meters of intricate paisleys, delicate florals, and perfectly aligned stripes in a matter of minutes. The combination of speed and precision meant that colorful, elaborately patterned fabrics were being made cheaper and more quickly than before.

Lightfoot had company instructions to experiment with aniline. He began by mixing an acid chloride of aniline, a pungent solution of equal parts pure hydrochloric acid and aniline, with some starch paste and chlorate of potash. He daubed a woodblock into his concoction and pressed it onto a swatch of cotton, but only faint traces of green stained the fabric. He tried again, this time putting the fabric through a copper roller printing machine. Though at first the results were the same disappointing pallid stains as the ones left by woodblocks, when Lightfoot returned 12 hours later, the cloth had turned deep green. The unexpected color change encouraged Lightfoot to keep experimenting. He remade his original aniline mixture, this time adding a little copper salt, and then printing a swatch. Next, he added a bit more aniline salt, and printed again. He continued going back and forth. At first the dye was pale green, a minty shade not far from pistachio ice cream, but it gradually deepened to a forest green over the course of a day. When Lightfoot rinsed in water the fabric of the darkest green he had achieved, it deepened to raven black.

Lightfoot didn't think much of his discovery. At the time, aniline was prohibitively expensive, so he saw his new dye as little more than a chemical curiosity. But in the same year that Lightfoot had chanced upon the black, Heinrich Caro, a German chemist working in Manchester, UK, was developing a new way to make aniline purple, and the process had unexpectedly left an inky black residue, which Caro began selling to fabric printers as a black dye-paste.

Both Caro's and Lightfoot's processes wreaked havoc on metal printing equipment. The salts used to make aniline black corroded the metal rollers, leaving streaky patterns all over the fabrics, but it did nothing harmful to wood blocks. The British industry had switched to high-tech roller printing but many European printing companies were still working with traditional woodblocks. So while the British market didn't immediately jump on aniline black, a buyer across the channel saw the potential and swiftly moved in.

J. J. Müller-Pack (the specious dye magnate from Basel, see *Magenta*, page 196), bought the rights to Caro's process first. Then, in 1863, he bought Lightfoot's aniline black process. Shortly after this, two French printers found a way to stop the solution corroding the metal printing machines, and Müller-Pack snapped up that patent, too, insisting that English, French, and American printers pay him royalties for making and using aniline black. But soon other chemists had created similar blacks, which they claimed were outside of Müller-Pack's patents, and while he finally won the battle in 1876, further patent battles and lawsuits ensued over the next quarter of a century. By 1900, 11 different patents for aniline black had been issued in America alone.

In the years between, aniline black had become hugely fashionable. According to one French dye house in 1877, "What was formerly a mark of mourning has become a novelty,"—its traditionally somber associations adding to its appeal as a wider trend. But alongside dyeing luxurious fabrics like cotton velvets, aniline black's financial value was tied to more practical wares; its resistance to sun-fading made it a popular dye for umbrellas and sun blinds.

In 1913—50-odd years after its discovery—the aniline black molecular puzzle that had stumped scientists for decades was finally solved and its chemical structure agreed. Twenty years earlier it would have been a groundbreaking discovery, but by that time the process had been perfected by trial and error and the patent wars had long since subsided. Soon after, cost-effective, efficient sulfur-black dyes hit the market, supplanting the compound that had been fought over for almost five decades. Aniline black was obsolete.

↓ A view of Becker's aniline and chemical dye works located in Flatlands, New York, 1917

Indigo

Other name. Indigo pure

Primary colorant. Indigotin

Colors. Blues

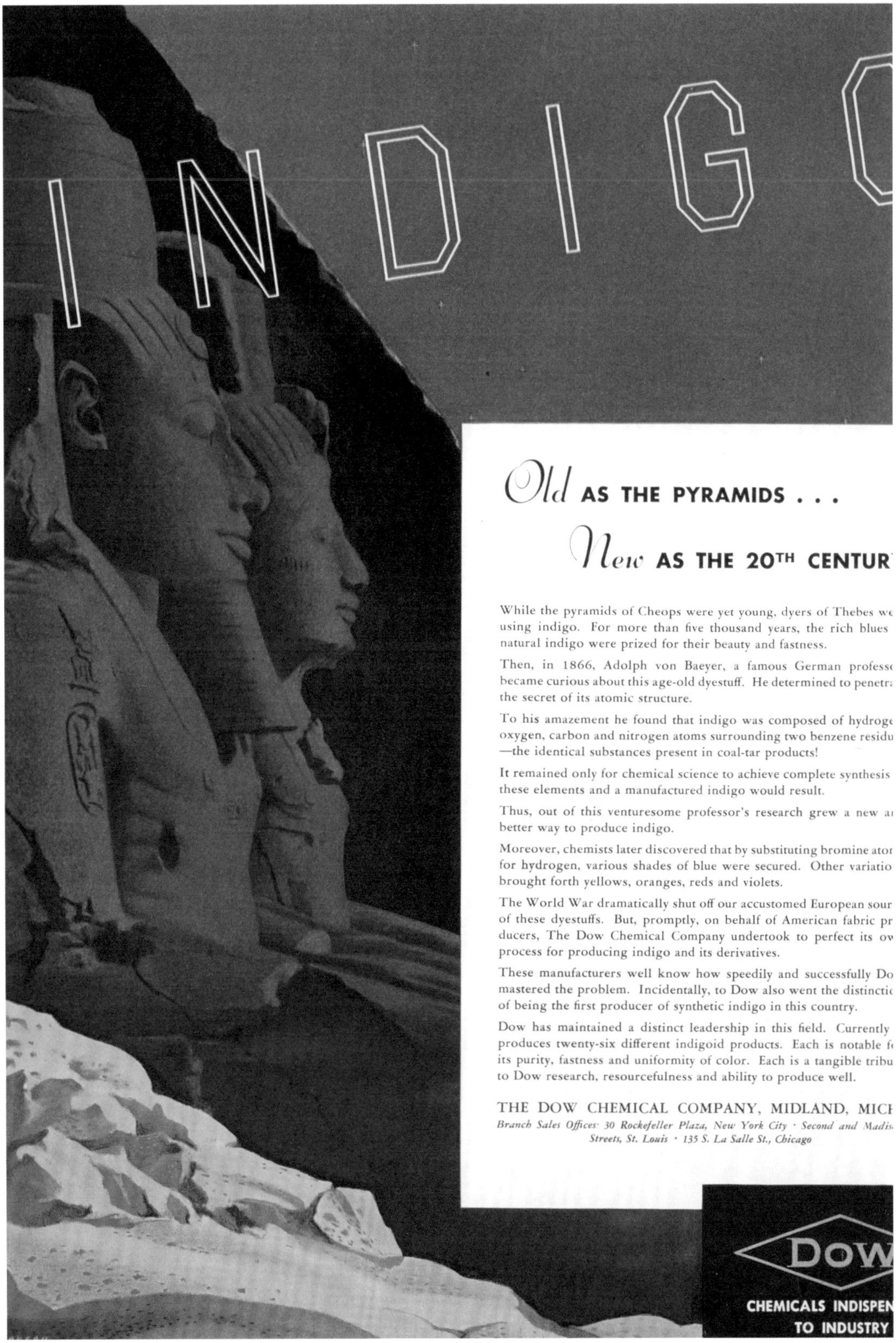
INDIGO
Old AS THE PYRAMIDS . . .
New AS THE 20TH CENTUR
While the pyramids of Cheops were yet young, dyers of Thebes we using indigo. For more than five thousand years, the rich blues natural indigo were prized for their beauty and fastness.
Then, in 1866, Adolph von Baeyer, a famous German professo became curious about this age-old dyestuff. He determined to penetra the secret of its atomic structure.
To his amazement he found that indigo was composed of hydroge oxygen, carbon and nitrogen atoms surrounding two benzene residu —the identical substances present in coal-tar products!
It remained only for chemical science to achieve complete synthesis these elements and a manufactured indigo would result.
Thus, out of this venturesome professor's research grew a new a better way to produce indigo.
Moreover, chemists later discovered that by substituting bromine ator for hydrogen, various shades of blue were secured. Other variatio brought forth yellows, oranges, reds and violets.
The World War dramatically shut off our accustomed European sour of these dyestuffs. But, promptly, on behalf of American fabric pr ducers, The Dow Chemical Company undertook to perfect its ow process for producing indigo and its derivatives.
These manufacturers well know how speedily and successfully Do mastered the problem. Incidentally, to Dow also went the distincti of being the first producer of synthetic indigo in this country.
Dow has maintained a distinct leadership in this field. Currently produces twenty-six different indigoid products. Each is notable f its purity, fastness and uniformity of color. Each is a tangible tribu to Dow research, resourcefulness and ability to produce well.
THE DOW CHEMICAL COMPANY, MIDLAND, MICH
Branch Sales Offices: 30 Rockefeller Plaza, New York City · Second and Madis Streets, St. Louis · 135 S. La Salle St., Chicago
DOW
CHEMICALS INDISPEN
TO INDUSTRY

← Brilliantly colored labels played an important role in the presentation of dyes. The customers, many of whom were illiterate, would recognize their preferred brand with the help of colors and symbols

↓ Portrait of Adolf von Baeyer, a recipient of the 1905 Nobel Prize in Chemistry, *c.*1884

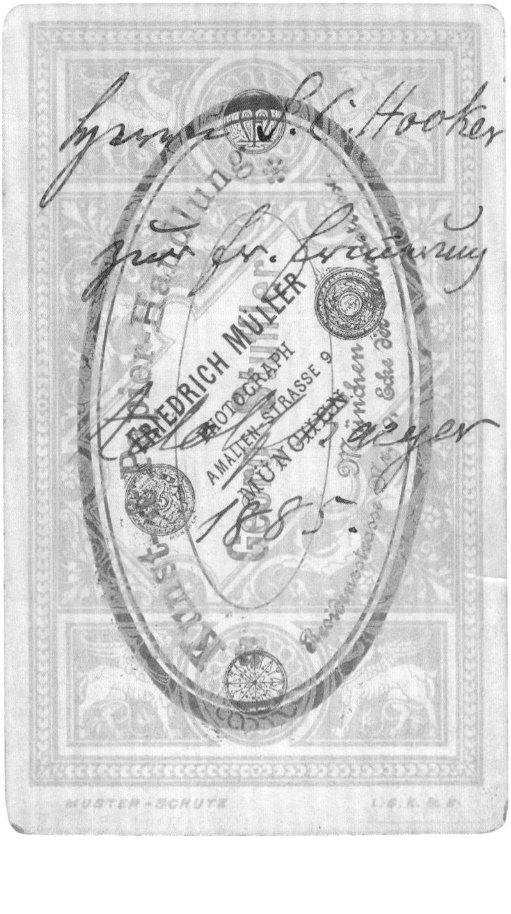

EUGENE SAPPER WAS A CLUMSY CHEMIST. A lab assistant at the German chemical company BASF, in 1890 Sapper was monitoring a boiling mix of naphthalene and sulfuric acid. The process was an expensive, dangerous, and slow way of oxidizing naphthalene, which was the first step in making synthetic indigo, a molecular copy of the world's most-used blue dye. Sapper lowered a thermometer in to take the solution's temperature and accidentally dropped it. The thermometer shattered; glass and mercury spilled into the mix. Sapper thought he was done for—until he noticed what the solution was doing; the reaction was speeding up. He had discovered that mercury worked as a catalyst for naphthalene oxidation. Like fellow chemist Perkin's accidental discovery of mauveine nearly 40 years earlier, Sapper had found the key to a new bestselling dye by chance.

The race to find a synthetic alternative to natural indigo had been on for some time. In 1880, future Nobel Prize winner Adolf Von Baeyer had cracked indigotin's molecular structure and had even managed to make indigo dye, but a process for making a synthetic indigo that was cheaper than its natural alternative continued to elude scientists. By 1890, BASF had been working on synthetic indigo for over a decade, pouring 18 million marks into its development (more than the company's capital value at the time) and had put their top chemists on the case. BASF's Indigo Pure, the first commercially viable synthetic indigo, wouldn't hit the market until 1897, but Sapper's discovery was a critical breakthrough.

When Indigo Pure finally hit the market it was met with a mixed response. Reviews from Germany, where it had been developed and was set to be an incredibly lucrative industry were, unsurprisingly, positive. Reviews from Britain, which still controlled natural indigo production in Bengal and Bihar, were far less so. The invention of synthetic indigo threatened the wealth of the British indigo industry, as well as the livelihood of the Indians working on plantations and in dye factories.

Critical accounts from the time shake their heads at the British indigo industry's reaction. After all, another invention of BASF, synthetic alizarin, had devastated the madder industries in France and Holland just 30 years before. Synthetic indigo had been in the works for decades—had the planters not seen the writing on the wall? Or were they just in denial?

Whatever the case, there was no way to stave off the influx of synthetic indigo, though some tried. Competitors accused BASF of fraud, claiming synthetic indigo wasn't indigo at all. British planters in India formed the Indigo Defence Association, hiring chemists to try to improve yields and processing methods. The British government mandated that army and navy uniforms be dyed with natural indigo from Bihar (meanwhile the German government mandated the use of synthetic indigo for its uniforms), and campaigners attacked the "blueness" of the new blue dye, leading to a centuries-long dispute over the quality of the color that is still going on today.

The blueness debate may have been propaganda by indigo planters, but there is something to it. While the indigotin in synthetic and natural indigo is identical, there are other colorants present in indigo plants. For example, natural indigo can contain "indigo red" (indirubin) and yellows in the form of flavonoids. There are also reports of "indigo brown" and "indigo gluten," tannins, and yet more colorants that dyers claim give natural indigo a richer result, adding depth and variation to natural indigo that synthetic indigo can't copy.

Despite the defamation attempts and protectionist trade policy, synthetic indigo started to flood the market. Since it relied on chemistry rather than climate and human labor, the end dye was more consistent and the price more competitive. It annihilated the British–Indian natural indigo industry. In the 1880s there were some 2,800 large indigo factories across Bihar and Bengal; by 1911, only 121 remained. In 1895–1896, the total value of British–Indian indigo production was £3,566,700, but by 1914 it had plummeted to £70,000—down 98 percent in just under 20 years. It was woad all over again (see page 58).

After the catastrophic crash of the natural indigo industry, some moments of respite followed in the coming decades. During the First World War, the allied forces imposed a naval blockade on Germany, stopping all exports, which meant the British–Indian dye sector temporarily bounced back. A second, smaller rebound during the Second World War meant that a small amount of Bengal indigo was still being traded to Britain into the 1950s. But the demand for natural indigo had permanently fallen, and in desperation the British indigo industry in Bihar tried to minimize its losses at the expense of the peasant farmers. The British planters increased rents, beat and imprisoned peasants to try and extract money, looted, and imposed illegal “taxes” on marriage and homes, among other things. The tension between British planters and Indian peasants was palpable, and in 1917 the deplorable conditions of the indigo farmers caught the attention of a certain pro-independence lawyer called Mahatma Gandhi, who traveled to North Bihar in a show of solidarity with the indigo peasants facing daily injustices. This was the first of many of Gandhi’s campaigns of non-violent resistance in India, and launched what would become a national movement for independence from British rule.

Synthetic indigo hasn’t been impervious to the fickle nature of fashion trends. The invention of other synthetic blues led to a steep decline in its use during the 20th century. But a saving grace came in the 1950s and ’60s when sales of blue jeans, popularized by movie stars like James Dean and Marlon Brando, started to gain serious traction. Denim has remained popular ever since, and, at present, synthetic indigo is responsible for the deep blues of around one billion pairs of jeans annually (and, in 2018, for the many hues of the blue dogs in Mumbai).

↓ An early export label for the Bayer dye product known as Indigo Blue, 1912

Kaleidoscopic Futures

SINCE THE INVENTION OF synthetic dyes 170 years ago, textile and dye production has increased exponentially. At the time of writing, aggressive levels of production show no signs of slowing down. In 2017, the number of times your average t-shirt or pair of jeans was worn before being donated or thrown away was down 36 percent down from a decade earlier, while during the same period clothing production itself roughly doubled. Many believe our brightly colored clothes are pushing resources to the brink.

There are several proposed solutions to reduce dye and textile industry pollution. Genetic engineering is being explored in a variety of ways, from changing cotton genes so that the fluffy bolls are blue, green, or red instead of light cream and therefore require no dye, to modifying common bacterial species to get them to produce dyes. Recently, biomolecular chemists injected DNA into a bacterium that naturally produces indigoidine, one of the building blocks of indigo. The gene that the chemists added propels the bacteria to assemble all the blocks needed to produce the blue dye, which was trialed on white cotton. Across the industry there is research and development on dye processes that reduce water use, ways to make new textiles from old ones (which reduces overall energy consumption and raw material use), and on the consumer side, high-street shops have started advertising clothes made from plastic bottles and recycled cotton blends as well as the (not-so-tech) solution of offering recycling programs for clothes (although what happens *after* your old t-shirt gets dropped in its allocated bin is often unclear).

The trouble is, it's really hard to know what is being done in earnest and what is greenwashing—a way for corporations to promote an eco-image without really following through. As for these new technologies, will they really have the impact necessary to temper the effects of centuries of industrial pollution? Is this research just a way to assuage ourselves as we face the realities of a warming climate? Though optimistic and well-intended, the innovations in dyeing may be perpetuating the very thing they are intended to counteract: the ongoing production of too much stuff.

I'd like to think that after discovering how rare and precious bright red and deep blue dyes used to be, you'll have gained a new appreciation for the ones already around your house and in your closet. Perhaps you'll try natural dyeing for yourself, sow some weld in your garden, or become the dreaded party guest who warns everyone that there are cochineal insects in the red velvet cake. Whatever you take away from this book, I hope you have a new sense of how color comes into the world, and that you'll share it with others. In the words of natural dyer Charllotte Kwon (see page 29), "action is hopeful."

→ DuPont Exhibition at the New York Museum of Science and Industry, Rockefeller Center, 1937

Building a Library on Natural Dyes

I've put together a few of my favorite books and resources that I used time and time again in my research for this one. If you're interested in reading more on the subject of dyeing, I'd suggest:

Cardon D. (2007) *Natural Dyes: Sources, Tradition, Technology and Science*. Archetype Publications, London.

Cardon's book is the product of decades worth of research and practical experience in dyeing. It's an encyclopedic tome of hundreds of dyes and their stories. If you only buy one book, it should be this one.

Balfour Paul J. (1998) *Indigo*. British Museum Press, London.

This seminal text on indigo is a beautiful and expansive deep-dive into a world of blue dye.

Boutrup J. and Ellis C. (2018) *The Art and Science of Natural Dyes*. Schiffer Publishing, Atglen, PA.

This book is a collaborative effort between a textile artist and a chemist. It has detailed explanations of the science behind natural dyes and it's waterproof (so an excellent handbook for your workshop).

Online Resources

Both Maiwa (maiwa.teachable.com) and Botanical Colors (botanicalcolors.com) offer well-researched, in-depth online resources. For more information about local and regenerative fiber systems, check out Fibershed (fibershed.org).

References

Abelshauser W., von Hippel W., Johnson J. A., and Stokes R. G. (2003) *German Industry and Global Enterprise: BASF: The History of a Company*. Cambridge University Press, Cambridge.

Adrosko R. J. (2012) *Natural Dyes and Home Dyeing*. Dover Publications,. Mineola, NY.

Alexa A. (2019) This ethereal raincoat is made out of algae based plastic. *Core 77*, 16 May.

Alighieri D. (trans. Cary H. F.) (1888) *Inferno*. George Bell, London.

Aljazeera (2021) Chile's desert dumping ground for fast fashion leftovers. *Aljazeera*, 8 November.

Amar Z., Gottlieb H., Varshavsky L., and Iluz D. (2005) The scarlet dye of the Holy Land. *BioScience* 55(12), pp. 1080–1083.

American Chemical Society (1995) *A National Historic Chemical Landmark: The First Nylon Plant*. American Chemical Society, Division of the History of Chemistry and the Office of Public Outreach, Washington, DC.

Appleton P. A. (2018) *A Forgotten Industry: The alum shale industry of north-east Yorkshire*. Boroughgate Books, Saltburn by the Sea.

Archibald A. (2021) Galling Ink! How the National Archives preserves millions of documents written in iron gall ink. National Archives. https://blog.nationalarchives.gov.uk/galling-ink-how-the-national-archives-preserves-millions-of-documents-written-in-iron-gall-ink/.

Arte Lana Della (trans. Cardon D.) (1418) Codex 2580. Bioblioteca Riccaridiana, Florence.

Avery W. T. (1940) The "Adoratio Purpurae" and the importance of imperial purple in the fourth century of the Christian Era. *Memoirs of the American Academy in Rome* 17, pp. 66–80.

Aygün Ç. Ö. (2020) The flesh eating stone: alum mining and trade in Asia Minor. In: Dallai L., Bianchi G., and Romana Stasolla F. (eds), *Alum Landscapes: Archaeology of Production and Network Economy*. All'Insegna del Giglio, Sesto Fiorentino, pp. 175–181.

Azami K., Hayashi T., Kusumi T., Ohmori K., and Suzuki K. (2019) Total synthesis of carthamin, a traditional natural red pigment. *Angewandte Chemie International Edition* 58(16), pp. 5321–5326.

Baboo B. and Goswami D. N. (2010) *Processing Chemistry and Applications of Lac*. Indian Council of Agricultural Research, New Delhi.

Balfour Paul J. (1997) *Indigo in the Arab World*. Curzon, London.

Balfour Paul J. (1998) *Indigo*. British Museum Press, London.

Ball P. (2001) *Bright Earth: The Invention of Colour*. Vintage Books, London.

Barber E. J. W. (1991) *Prehistoric Textiles: The Development of Cloth in the Neolithic and Bronze Ages with Special Reference to the Aegean*. Princeton University Press, Princeton.

BASF (2022) Looking back over our history: Important Innovations at BASF. https://www.basf.com/gb/en/who-we-are/innovation/our-innovations/historic-innovations.html.

Bass-Krueger M. (2019) Vogue Encyclopaedia: the history of denim jeans. *Vogue*, 10 April.

Bayer E. (2019) The mycelium revolution is upon us. *Scientific American*, 1 July.

BBC Staff (2019) Sussex fake saffron discovery leads to £750,00 haul. *BBC News*, 6 August.

Beaujour F. (1800) *Tableau du Commerce de la Grèce*. Chez Ant.-Aug Renouard, Paris.

Beckert S. (2014) *Empire of Cotton: A Global History*. Penguin Random House, New York.

Beckman J. (1846) *A History of Inventions, Discoveries, and Origins, vol 1*. Henry G. Bohn, London.

Beeler J. (2022) Mushroom Color Atlas. https://mushroomcoloratlas.com.

Bell S. (2018) Oregan grape, a traditional Sinixt dye. Stravaigin Yarn Co. https://www.stravaigin-yarnco.com.

Bender M. (2021) Engineered bacteria produce a rainbow of colors. *Scientific American*, 1 September.

Berbers S. V. J., Tamburini D., van Bommel M. R., and Dyer J. (2019) Historical formulations of lake pigments and dyes derived from lac: a study of compositional variability. *Dyes and Pigments* 170.

Bernat i Roca M. (1995) *El "Ill mesters de la llana" paraires, teixidors de llan I tintorers a Ciutat de Mallorca (s. XIV—XVII)*. Institute d'Estudis Baleàrics. Palma.

Bertolet C. E. (2016) *Chaucer, Gower, Hoccleve and the Commercial Practices of Late Fourteenth-Century London*. Taylor and Francis, London.

Bessette A. E. and Bessette A. R. (2001) *The Rainbow Beneath My Feet: A Mushroom Dyer's Field Guide*. Syracuse University Press, Syracuse, NY.

Biringuccio V (trans. Smith C.S. and Grudi M.T.) (1959) *The Pirotechnia of Vannoccio Biringuccio*. Dover Publications, New York.

Bogensperger L. (2017) Purple and its various kinds in documentary papyri. In: Gaspa S, Michel C., and Nosch, M. (eds), *Textile Terminologies from the Orient to the Mediterranean and Europe, 1000 BC to 1000 AD*. Zea Books, Lincoln, NE, pp. 235–249.

Böhmer H. and Karadag R. (2003) New dye research on Palmyra textiles. *Dyes in History and Archaeology* 19, pp. 88–93.

Borelli-Persson L. (2018) thinking deeply about pink at the museum at FIT. *Vogue*, 7 September.

Bolton E. M., Bolton Holloway J., and Casselman K.L (eds) (1997) *Lichens for Vegetable Dyeing*. Robin and Russ Handweavers, McMinnville, OR.

Bota Totxo M. (1985) La llegenda de la Urxella. *Perlas y Cuevas*, 20 April.

Brackman B. (2009) *Clues in the Calico: A Guide to Identifying and Dating Antique Quilts*. C&T Publishing, Concord, CA.

Brennan S. (2017) A natural history of the wedding dress. *Jstor Daily*, 27 September.

Brundage J.A. (1987) Sumptuary laws and prostitution in Late Medieval Italy. *Journal of Medieval History* 13(4), pp. 343–355.

Brunello F. (trans. Hickey B.) (1973) *The Art of Dyeing in the History of Mankind*. Neri Pozza Editore, Vicenza.

Buchanan R. (1999) *A Weaver's Garden: Growing Plants for Natural Dyes and Fibers*. Dover Publications, Mineola.

Bulletin of Miscellaneous Information (1902) Woad. (Isatis tinctoria, L.) *Bulletin of Miscellaneous Information (Royal Botanic Gardens, Kew)*, 1902(1), pp. 15–17.

Camille M. A. and Espejjo-Saavedra R. (1996) Historical geography of the Belizean logwood trade. *Yearbook (Conference of Latin Americanist Geographers)* vol. 22. University of Texas Press, Austin, TX, pp. 77–85.

Campbell L., Dunkerton J., Kirby J., and Monnas L. (2001). Two panels by Ercol de' Roberti and the identification of "Veluto Morello". *National Gallery Technical Bulletin* 22.

Campbell Thompson R. (ed) (1934) An Assyrian chemist's vademecum. *Journal of the Royal Asiatic Society of Great Britain and Ireland*, pp. 771–785.

Cardon D. (1999) La garrigue, monde de l'écarlate. *Études rurales* 151–152, pp. 33–44.

Cardon D., Brémaud I., Quye A., and Balfour-Paul J. (2020) Exploring colors from the past: in the steps of eighteenth-century dyers from France and England. *Textile Museum Journal* 47, pp. 9–18.

Carr G. (2005) Woad, tattooing and identifying later Iron Age and Early Roman Britain. *Oxford Journal of Archaeology* 24(3), pp. 273–292.

Casselman K. L. (1994) Lichen dyes: preparation and dyeing. *Maine Naturalist* 2(2), pp. 105–110.

Casselman K. L. D. (1999) Lichen dyes and dyeing: A critical bibliography of the European and North American literature in a culturally marginalized field. MA thesis. Saint Mary's University, Halifax, NS.

Casselman K. D. and Terada T. (2012) The politics of purple: dyes from shellfish and lichens. *Textile Society of America Symposium Proceedings*. University of Nebraska, Lincoln, NE.

Castro R., Adelaide M., and Melo M. (2016) Interpreting lac dye in medieval written sources: new knowledge from the reconstruction of recipes relating to illuminations in Portuguese manuscripts. In: Eyb-Green S., Townsend J., Pilz K., Kroustallis S., and van Leeuwen I. (eds), *Sources in Art Technology: Back to Basics*. Archetype, London, pp. 88–99.

Chapman M. A. and Burke J. M. (2007) DNA sequence diversity and the origin of cultivated safflower (*Carthamus tinctorius* L.; Asteraceae). *BMC Plant Biology* 7(60).

Chaucer G. and Benson L. D. (eds) (1986) *The Riverside Chaucer*. Oxford University Press. Oxford.

Chenciner R. (2000) *Madder Red: A History of Luxury and Trade*. Routledge, Milton Park.

Cline E. L. and Lanfranchi M. (2021) *Cotton: A Case Study in Misinformation*. Transformers Foundation, New York, NY.

Cohen A. and Norman E. S. (2018) Renegotiating the Columbia River Treaty: transboundary governance and indigenous rights. *Global Environmental Politics* 18(4), pp. 4–24.

Colwall D. (1677) An account of the English alum-works, communicated by Daniel Colwall esquire. *Philosophical Transactions*. (12) pp. 1052–1056.

Clow A. and Clow N. L. (1970) *The Chemical Revolution: A Contribution to Social Technology*. Books for Libraries Press, Freeport, NY.

Cooksey C. J. (2019) The red insect dyes: carminic, kermesic, and laccaic acids and their derivatives. *Biotech Histochem* 94(2), pp. 100–107.

Cooksey C. J. (2013) Tyrian purple: the first four thousand years. *Science Progress* 96(2), pp. 171–186.

Cooper T. (1815) *A Practical Treatise on Dyeing, and Callicoe Printing, Exhibiting the Processes in the French, German, English, and American Practice of Fixing Colours on Woollen, Cotton, Silk, and Linen* Thomas Dobson, Philadelphia, PA.

Cowie E. E. (2008) Colwall, Daniel. *Oxford Dictionary of National Biography*. Oxford University Press, Oxford.

Craig A. K. (1969) Logwood as a factor in the settlement of British Honduras. *Caribbean Studies* 9(1), pp. 53–62.

Crawford S. D. (2015) Lichens used in traditional medicine. In: Ranković B. (ed.), *Lichen Secondary Metabolites*. Springer, New York, NY.

Crookes W. (1874) Patents. *Chemical News and Journal of Industrial Science*, 20 July, pp. 22.

Cunningham A. B., Made Maduarta I., Howe J., Ingram W., and Jansen S. (2011) Hanging by a thread: natural metallic mordant processes in traditional Indonesian textiles. *Economic Botany* 65(3), pp. 241–259.

Cushman G. T. (2013) *Guano and the Opening of the Pacific World: A Global Ecological History*. Cambridge University Press, Cambridge.

Dana W. B. (ed.) (1866) *Merchants' Magazine and Commercial Review* 55.

Dawson W. R. (1949) Anastasi, Sallier, and Harris and their papyri. *Journal of Egyptian Archaeology*, (35) pp. 158–166.

Delshad E., Yousefi M., Sassanezhad P., Rakhshandeh H., and Ayati Z. (2018) Medical uses of *Carthamus tinctorius* L. (safflower): a comprehensive review from traditional medicine to modern medicine. *Electron Physician* 10(4), pp. 6672–6681.

Deveoglu O. and Karadag R. (2019) A review on the flavonoids—a dye source. *International Journal of Advances in Engineering and Pure Science* 3, pp. 188–200.

Diaz G., Miranda I., Sartori S. K., de Rezende D. C., and Nogueira M. A. (2018) Anthraquinones: an overview. *Studies in Natural Products Chemistry* 58, pp. 313–338.

Dickson D. (2014) *The People's Government: An Introduction to Democracy*. Cambridge University Press, Cambridge.

Domagalska B. W. (2010) Safflower (*Carthamus tinctorius*)—forgotten cosmetic plant. *Cosmetology Today*, pp. 6–9.

Donald G. (2013) *The Accidental Scientist: The Role of Chance and Luck in Scientific Discovery*. Michael O'Mara Books, London.

Donkin R. A. (1977) Spanish red: an ethnogeography study of cochineal and the *Opuntia* cactus. *Transactions of the American Philosophical Society* 67(5), pp. 1–84.

Ducol Organics (2022) Colourful landmarks. Ducol Organics. https://www.ducol.com/about_us_landmarks.html

Duhamel du Monceau H. L. *et al.* (1739-1741) Observations and experiments with madder-root, which has the faculty of tinging the bones of living animals of a red colour. *Philosophical Transactions* 41, pp. 390–406.

Dusengemungu L., Kasali G., Gwanama C., and Ochieng Ouma K. (2020) Recent advances in biosorption of Ccopper and cobalt by filamentous fungi. *Frontiers in Microbiology* 11, article 582016.

Dyer J., Tamburini D., and Sotiropoulou S. (2018) The identification of lac as a pigment in ancient Greek polychromy—the case of a Hellenistic oinochoe from Canosa di Puglia. *Dyes and Pigments* 149, pp. 122–132.

Eamon W. (1984) Arcana disclosed: the advent of printing, the books of secrets tradition and the development of experimental science in the sixteenth century. *History of Science; An Annual Review of Literature, Research and Teaching* 22(2), pp. 111–150.

Eamon W. (1985) Books of Secrets in Medieval and Early Modern Science. *Sudhoffs Archive* 69(1), pp. 26–49.

Eastaugh N., Walsh V., and Chaplin T. (2008) Pigment Compendium: *A Dictionary and Optical Microscopy of Historical Pigments*. Butterworth-Heinemann, Oxford.

Edelstein S. M. (1966) Dyeing fabrics in sixteenth-century Venice. *Technology and Culture* 7(3), pp. 395–397.

Edelstein S. M. and Borghetty H. C. (eds) (1969) *The Plictho of Gioventura Rosetti: Instructions in the Art of the Dyers Which Teaches the Dyeing of Woolen Clothe, Linens, Cottons, and Silk by the great Art as Well as the Common*. MIT Press. Cambridge, MA.

Edmonds J. (2012) *Medieval Textile Dyeing*. Self-published.

Ellen MacArthur Foundation (2017) *A New Textiles Economy: Redesigning fashion's future*. Ellen MacArthur Foundation, Circular Fiber Initiative, Isle of Wight.

Ellis A. (1798) *The Country Dyer's Assistant*. E. Merriam, Brookfield, MA.

Emsley J. (2006) *The Elements of Murder: A History of Poison*. Oxford University Press, Oxford.

Fagin D. (2014) *Tom's River: A Story of Science and Salvation*. Bantam Books, New York, NY.

Feeser A. (2013) *Red, White, and Black Make Blue: Indigo in the Fabric of Colonial South Carolina Life*. University of Georgia Press, Athens, GA.

Frame M. (1995) *Ancient Peruvian Mantles, 300 B.C.—A.D. 200*. The Metropolitan Museum of Art, New York, NY.

Frazer J. (2013) Wonderful things: the hidden beauty of the horse dung fungus. *Scientific American*, 24 August.

Freudenberger H. (1963) Fashion sumptuary laws and business. *Business History Review* 37(1/2), pp. 37–48.

Frutuoso G. (1873) *As Saudades Da Terra*. Typ. Funchalense, Funchal.

Fu Y. and Viraraghavan T. (2001) Fungal decolorization of dye wastewaters: a review. *Bioresource Technology* 79(3), pp. 252–262.

Fury A. (2013) Impress of an empress: the influence of Eugénie on luxury style is still felt today. *The Independent*, 18 September.

Gage J. (1999) *Color and Culture: Practice and Meaning from Antiquity to Abstraction*. University of California Press, Berkeley, CA.

Garfield S. (2000) *Mauve: How One Man Invented a Colour that Changed the World*. Canongate Books, Edinburgh.

Gibson A. J. (1942) The story of lac. *Journal of the Royal Society of Arts* 90(4611), pp. 319–335.

Gilmore M. R. (1933) *Some Chippewa Uses of Plants*. University of Michigan Press, Ann Arbor, MI, pp. 131.

Glick T. F. (2014) Alum. In: *Medieval Science, Technology, and Medicine*. Taylor and Francis, Oxford, pp. 32.

Gossman L. (2000) *Basel in the Age of Burckhardt: A Study in Unseasonable Ideas*. University of Chicago Press, Chicago, IL.

Govan F. (2010) Spanish prostitutes ordered to wear reflective vests for their own safety. *The Telegraph*, 25 October.

Gupta A. D. (2011) Science and modern India: an institutional history, c.1784–1947, Vol. XV, part 4. In: Chattopadhyaya D. P. (ed.), *History of Science, Philosophy and Culture in Indian Civilization.* Pearson Education, New Delhi.

Greenfield A. B. (2005) *A Perfect Red: Empire, Espionage, and the Quest for the Color of Desire.* Doubleday, London.

Hacke M. 2009) Weighted silk: history, analysis and conservation. *Studies in Conservation* 54(1), pp. 2–15.

Hamilton H.C and Falconer W. (1903) *The Geography of Strabo. Literally Translated, with Notes, in Three Volumes.* George Bell, London.

Hansen C. (2021) Century-old textiles woven from fascinating fungus. *Scientific American*, 1 June.

Hansen H. (2011) The quest for quercitron: revealing the story of a forgotten dye. MA thesis. University of Delaware, DE.

Haude M. E. (2022) *Prickly Pear Blood.* United States Library of Congress, Washington, DC.

Hellot J. (1789) *The art of dyeing wool, silk, and cotton. Translated from the French of M. Hellot, M. Macquer, and M. le Pileur D'Apligny.* Baldwin, London.

Herbert M. (1994) An infancy narrative of Saint Ciarán. *Proceedings of the Harvard Celtic Colloquium* 14, pp. 1–8.

Hindustan Times (2020) Prayagraj's Lakshagriha, said to be Mahabharat-era site, to get research centre. *Hindustan Times*, 23 September.

Hoad J. (1987) *This is Donegal Tweed.* Shoestring Publications, Donegal.

Hofenk de Graaf J. H. and Van Bommel M. R. (2001) Dyestuff analysis of the Central Asian woolen textiles. In: Bunker E. C., Keller D., and Schorta R. (eds), *Fabulous Creatures from the Desert Sands: Central Asian Woolen Textiles from the Second Century* BC *to the Second Century* AD, vol. 10. Abigg Siftung, Riggisberg, pp. 137–150.

Hofmann-de Keijzer R., Van Bommel M. R., Joosten I., and Hartl A. (2013) The colours and dyeing techniques of prehistoric textiles from the salt mines of Hallstatt. In: Gromer K., Kern A., and Reschreiter H. (eds), *Textiles from Hallstatt. Weaving Culture and Bronze Age Salt Mines.* Archaeolingua, Budapest, pp. 135–162.

Holst S. (2011) *Phoenician Secrets: Exploring the Ancient Mediterranean.* Santorini Books, Los Angeles.

Holm D. (2014) Why these colors don't run: dyeing the Star Spangled Banner. National Museum of American History Behring Centre. https://americanhistory.si.edu/blog/2014/04/why-these-colors-dont-run-dyeing-the-star-spangled-banner.html.

Homer and Butler S. (1898) *The Iliad of Homer. Rendered into English prose for the use of those who cannot read the original.* Longmans, Green, London.

Hoskins J. (1989) Why do ladies sing the blues? Indigo dyeing, cloth production and gender symbolism in Kodi. In: Schneider J. and Weiner A.B. (eds.), *Cloth and Human Experience.* Smithsonian Institution Press, Washington, DC, pp. 141–173.

Hou K. and LaMantia B. (2022) The 50 most classic lipstick colors of all time. *New York Magazine*, 31 October.

House J. E. and House K. A. (2010) *Descriptive Inorganic Chemistry*, 2nd edn. Elsevier, London, pp. 17–61.

Howard G. (2003) *Arsenic, Drinking-water and Health Risk Substitution in Arsenic Mitigation: A Discussion Paper.* World Health Organization, Geneva.

Hulme A. N., McNab H., Peggie D. A., and Quye A. (2017) The chemical characteristics by HPLC-PDA and HPLC-EESI-MS of unaged and aged fibre samples dyed with sawwort (*Serratula tinctoria L.*). In: Atkinson J. K. (eds), *The Diversity of Dyes in History and Archaeology.* Archetype, London, pp. 374–382.

Hunt A. (1996) *Governance of the Consuming Passions: A History of Sumptuary Law.* Macmillan Press, Houndmills.

Huun K. (2021) Textile waste. University of Colorado Boulder, Environmental Centre, Division of Student Affairs. https://www.colorado.edu/ecenter/2021/10/05/textile-waste.

Illustrated London News (1858) Fashions for April. 3 April, pp. 22.

Inalcik H. (1960) Bursa and the commerce of the Levant. *Journal of the Economic and Social History of the Orient* 3(2), pp. 131–147.

Iqbal N. F. (2013) Ambivalent blues: woad and indigo in tension in early modern Europe. *Constellations (University of Alberta Student Journal)*, 4(1).

Jackson L. (2014) *Dirty Old London: The Victorian Fight Against Filth.* Yale University Press, London.

James M., Reifarth N., Mukherjee A., Crump M., Gates P., Sandor P., Roberston F., Pfálzner P., and Evershed R. (2009) High prestige royal purple dyed textile from the Bronze Age royal tomb at Qatna, Syria. *Antiquity* 83(322), pp. 1109–1118.

Jansen P. C. M. and Cardon D. (eds) (2005) *Dyes and tannins.* PROTA Foundation, Wageningen.

Jeffreys D. (2010) *Hell's Cartel: IG Farben and the Making of Hitler's War Machine.* Henry Holt, New York, NY.

Jensen L. B. (1963) Royal purple of Tyre. *Journal of Near Eastern Studies* 22(2), pp. 104

Jensen W. B. (eds) (trans. Caley E. R.) (2008) *The Leyden and Stockholm Papyri: Greco-Egyptian Chemical Documents From the Early 4th Century AD.* Oesper Collections in the History of Chemistry, University of Cincinnati, Cincinnati, OH.

Johansen K. (2008) Perfumed textiles. *Textile Society of America Symposium Proceedings.* University of Nebraska, Lincoln, NE.

Jones S., Kern A. L., and Watanabe K. (2020) *A Kamigata Anthology: Literature from Japan's Metropolitan Centers,* 1600-1750. University of Hawai'i Press, Honolulu.

Jonson B. (1974) *Ben Jonson: The Alchemist.* Yale University Press, New Haven, CT.

Johnston W. T. (2007) The discovery of aniline and the origin of the term "aniline dye". *Biotechnic & Histochemistry* 83(2), pp. 83–87.

Joseph A. (2014) "A wizard of silks and tulle": Charles Worth and the queer origins of couture. *Victorian Studies* 56(2), pp. 251–279.

Kassinger R. (2003) *Dyes: From Sea Snails to Synthetics.* Twenty-first Century Books. Minneapolis, MN.

Kim J. (2010) Indian peasants in the Champaign campaign for rights, 1917. Global Nonviolent Action Database. https://nvdatabase.swarthmore.edu/content/indian-peasants-champaran-campaign-rights-1917.

Kling B. B. (1966) *The Blue Mutiny, The Indigo Disturbances in Bengal, 1859–1862.* University of Philadelphia Press, Philadelphia.

Kok A. (1966) A short history of the orchil dyes. *The Lichenologist* 3(2), pp. 248–272.

Knick Harley C. (1998) Cotton textile prices and the Industrial Revolution. *Economic History Review* 1(41), pp. 49–83.

Kvavadze E., Bar-Yosef O., Belfer-Cohen A., Boaretto E., Jakeli N., Matskevich Z., and Meshveliani T. (2009) 30,000-year-old wild flax fibers. *Science* 326(5951), pp. 366.

LaBerge M. (2018) The heart of the madder: an important prehistorical pigment and its botanical and cultural roots. MSc thesis. University of Wisconsin-Milwaukee.

Lacey A. and Sui C. (2015) Asia's deadly secret: the scourge of the betel nut. *BBC News*, 22 March.

Lakwete A. (2005) *Inventing the Cotton Gin Machine and Myth in Antebellum America.* John Hopkins University Press, Baltimore, MD.

Lambert B. and Pajic M. (2014) Drapery in exile: Edward III, Colchester and the Flemings, 1351-1467. *Journal of the Historical Association* 99(338), pp. 733–753.

Landi S. (2012) *Textile Conservator's Manual.* Taylor and Francis, London.

Leed D. (trans.) Shambles S.N. (1605) *A Profitable Booke, declaring dyers approved remedies to take out spots and stains in silks, velvets, linen, and woolen clothes ...* Thomas Purfoot, London.

Leggett W. F. (1944) *Ancient and Medieval Dyes.* Chemical Publishing Company, Brooklyn, NY.

Leong E. and Rankin A. (2011) Introduction: secrets and knowledge. In Leong E. and Rankin A (eds), *Secrets and Knowledge in Medicine and Science, 1500-1800*. Routledge, London.

Leuchs J. C. and Péclet E. (1829) *Traité complet des propriétés, de la preparation et de l'emploi des matières tinctoriales et des couleurs*. De Malher, Paris.

Lightfoot J. (1871) *The Chemical History and Progress of Aniline Black*. Lower House, Burnley.

Liles J. N. (1990) *The Art and Craft of Natural Dyeing: Traditional Recipes for Modern Use*. University of Tennessee Press, Knoxville, TN.

Lillethun A. (2008) Back silk, brown silk: China and beyond—traditional practice meets fashion. *Textile Society of America Symposium Proceedings*. University of Nebraska, Lincoln, NE.

Liu J., Mouri., C., Laursen R., Zhao F., Zhou Y., and Li W. (2013) Characterization of dyes in ancient textiles from Yingpan, Xinjiang. *Journal of Archaeological Science* 40(12), pp. 4444–4449.

Lucejko J. J., Vedeler M., and Degano I. (2021) Textile dyes from Gokstad Viking ship's grave. Pigments and dyes in archaeological and historical objects—scientific analyses and conservation challenges. *Heritage* 4(3), pp. 2278–2286.

Luhanko D. and Neumüller K. (2018) *Indigo: Cultivate, Dye, Create*. Pavilion Books, London.

Macdonald F. J. (1994) *Crowdie and Cream and Other Stories: Memories of a Hebridean Childhood*. Warner Books, New York, NY.

McDonald K. P. (2018) "Sailors from the woods": logwood cutting and the spectrum of piracy. In: Head D (eds), *The Golden Age of Piracy: The Rise, Fall, and Enduring Popularity of Pirates*. University of Georgia Press, Athens, GA, pp. 50–74.

McFarling U. L. (2019) Making ink from oak galls. Verso – The blog of the Huntington Library, Art Museum, and Botanical Gardens. https://huntington.org/verso/2019/05/making-ink-oak-galls.

McGinn T. A. J. (2003) *Prostitution, Sexuality, and the Law in Ancient Rome*. Oxford University Press, Oxford.

Mackay M. (2003) Traditional natural dyeing using crotal. *Biotechnic and Histochemistry* 78(6) pp. 309–311.

Maier M. B. (2017) Celts: *A History from the Earliest Times to the Present*. Edinburgh University Press, Edinburgh.

Mairet E. M. (1917) *Vegetable Dyes: Being a Book of Recipes and Other Information Useful to the Dyer*. Faber and Faber, London.

Malkin E. (2017) An insect's colorful gift, treasured by kings and artists. *The New York Times*, 27 November.

Malloch S. V. J. (2004) The death of Ptolemy of Mauretania. *Historia: Seitschrift für Alte Geschichte* 53(1), pp. 38–45.

Maraini F. (2021) Marco Polo. Encyclopaedia Britannica. https://www.britannica.com/biography/Marco-Polo

Marcotti G. (1881) *Un mercanto fiorentino e la sua famiglia nel secolo XV*. Tipografia di G. Barbèra, Florence.
Marin-Aguilera B., Iacono F., and Gleba M. (2019) Colouring the Mediterranean: production and consumption of purple-dyed textiles in pre-Roman times. *Journal of Mediterranean Archaeology* 31(2), pp. 127–154.

Marlow Taylor G. (2015) *The Alchemy of Al-Razi: A Translation of the "Book of Secrets"*. CreateSpace, Scotts Valley, CA.

Matrícula de tributos (Tribute Roll) (1522–1530). Author and place of publication not identified.

Matsiko M. (2020) Alum adjuvant discovery and potency. Nature Portfolio. https://www.nature.com/articles/d42859-020-00011-w.

May J., Hall A. R., and Van Der Veen M. (1993) Woad and the Britons painted blue. *Oxford Journal of Archaeology* 12(3), pp. 367–371.

Meier M. (1997) Müller Pack, Johann Jackob. *Neue Deutsche Biographie*, vol. 18. Bavarian Academy of Sciences and Humanities, Munich, p. 507.

Michel R. H., Lazar J., McGovern P. E. (1992) Indigoid dyes in Peruvian and Coptic textiles of the University Museum of Archaeology and Anthropology. *Archeomaterials* 6(1), pp. 69–83.

Miller J. E. and Reagan B. M (1989) Degradation in weighted and unweighted historic silks. *Journal of the American Institute for Conservation* 28(2), pp. 97–115.

Miller J. R. (2012) Residential schools in Canada. *The Canadian Encyclopaedia*. https://www.thecanadianencyclopedia.ca/en/article/residential-schools.

Ministry of Culture, Government of India (2022) Textiles of Nagaland. Indira Gandhi National Center for the Arts. https://ignca.gov.in/divisionss/janapada-sampada/northeastern-regional-centre/textiles-of-nagaland/.

Mitsui T. (trans. Crawcour E.S.) (1961) Some observations on merchants (1728). *Transactions of the Asiatic Society of Japan* 3(8).

Monnas L. (2014). Some medieval colour terms for textiles. In: Owen Crocker G. R. and Netherton R. (eds), *Medieval Clothing and Textiles*, vol. 10. Boydell Press, Woodbridge, pp. 25-58.

Morris P. J. T. and Travis A. S. (1992) A history of the international dyestuff industry. *American Dyestuff Reporter* 81(11).

Mnkandla S. M. and Otomo P. V. (2021) Effectiveness of mycofiltration for removal of contaminants from water: a systematic review protocol. *Environmental Evidence* 10(17).

Mukerjee R. (1937) Caste and social change in India. *American Journal of Sociology* 43(3), pp. 377–390.

Müller-Maatsch J. and Gras C. (2016) The "carmine problem" and potential alternatives. In: Carle R. and Schwieggert R. M. (eds), *Handbook on Natural Pigments in Food and Beverages*. Woodhead Publishing, Cambridge, pp. 385–428.

Mundy S. (2017) Blue dogs of Mumbai expose poor pollution controls. *Financial Times*, 28 August.

National Geographic. (2017) Blue dogs spotted in India—what's causing it? | National Geographic. *YouTube*. https://www.youtube.com/watch?v=-Vkx5zlkK08.

National Trust (2022) *How Alum Shaped The Yorkshire Coast*. https://web.archive.org/web/20211212212710/http://www.nationaltrust.org.uk/yorkshire-coast/features/how-alum-shaped-the-yorkshire-coast.

Nesbitt M. and Prance G. (eds) (2012) *The Cultural History of Plants*. Taylor and Francis, London.

Nieto-Galan A. (2013) *Colouring Textiles: A History of Natural Dyestuffs in Industrial Europe*. Springer, Heidelberg.

O'Connor K. (2011) *Lycra: How a Fiber Shaped America*. Taylor and Francis, London.

Ortiz-Hidalgo C. and Pina-Oviedo S. (2019) Hematoxylin: Mesoamerica's gift to histopathology. Palo de Campeche (logwood Tree), pirates' most desired treasure and irreplaceable tissue stain. International Journal of Surgical Pathology 27(1), pp. 4–14.

Palkina K. A., Ipatova D. A., Shakhova E. S., Balakireva A. V., and Marika N. M. (2021) Therapeutic potential of hispidin—fungal and plant polyketide. *Journal of Fungi* 7(5), pp. 323.

Pan Y., Xunan Y., Chen, X., Xu M., and Sun G. (2017). The right mud: studies in the mud-coating technique of gambiered Guangdong silk. *Applied Clay Science* 135, pp. 516–520.

Panche A.N., Diwan A.D., and Chandra S.R. (2016) Flavanoids: an overview. *Journal of Nutritional Science* 5(47).

Partridge E. (2006) Origins: *A Short Etymological Dictionary of Modern English*. Taylor and Francis, London.

Pastoureau M. (2008) *Black: The History of a Color*. Princeton University Press, Princeton, NJ.

Pastoureau M. (2017) *Red: The History of a Color*. Princeton University Press, Princeton, NJ.

Pastoureau M. (2018) *Blue: The History of a Color*. Princeton University Press, Princeton, NJ.

Pastoureau M. (2019) *Yellow: The History of a Color*. Princeton University Press, Princeton, NJ.

Payne E. E. (2007) The Craftsmen of the Neo-Babylonian Period: A Study of the Textile and Metal Workers of the Eanna Temple. PhD dissertation. Yale University, Cambridge, MA.

Perkin W. H. (1879) The history of alizarin & allied colouring matters and their production from coal tar. *Journal of the Society of Arts*, 30 May.

Phipps C. (2015) *No Wonder You Wonder! Great Inventions and Scientific Mysteries*. Springer, New York, NY.

Phipps E. (2010) *Cochineal Red: The Art History of a Color*. Metropolitan Museum of Art, New York, NY.

Phipps E. and Shibayama N. (2010) Tracing cochineal through the collection of the Metropolitan Museum. *Textile Society of America Symposium Proceedings*. University of Nebraska, Nebraska, NE.

Piemontese A. (1615) *The Secrets of Alexis: Containing Many Excellent Remedies Against Divers Diseases, Wounds, and Other Accidents. With the Manner to Make Distillations, Parfumes and Meltings*. R. Meighen, London.

Pliny the Elder (trans. Bostock J. and Riley H.) (2020) *The Natural History of Pliny*. Henry G. Bohn, London.

Popova M. (2011) *Harris Tweed: From Land to Street*. Frances Lincoln, London.

Polo M. (trans. Murray H.) (1847) *The Travels of Marco Polo*. Oliver and Boyd, Edinburgh.

Postrel V. (2020) *The Fabric of Civilization: How Textiles Made the World*. Basic Books, New York, NY.

Priest-Dorman C. (2002) "A grass that grows in Bologna": dyeing with weld in the Middle Ages. Paper prepared for Colour Congress 2022, Iowa State University, Ames, IA.

Punch (1859) The mauve measles. *Punch, or the London Charivari*, August 20, pp. 81.

Quataert D. (1997) Clothing laws, state, and society in the Ottoman Empire, 1720–1829. *International Journal of Middle East Studies* 29(3), pp. 403–425.

Ranson B. (2019) The true cost of colour: The impact of textile dyes on water systems. Fashion Revolution. https://www.fashionrevolution.org/the-true-cost-of-colour-the-impact-of-textile-dyes-on-water-systems/.

Rawson C. (1899) The cultivation and manufacture of indigo in Bengal. *Journal of the Society of Dyers and Colourists* 15(7), pp. 166–177.

Reed P. (1992) The British chemical industry and the indigo trade. *British Journal for the History of Science* 25(1), pp. 113–125.

Regan H. (2020) Asian rivers are turning black. And our colorful closets are to blame. CNN Style. https://edition.cnn.com/style/article/dyeing-pollution-fashion-intl-hnk-dst-sept/index.html.

Reinhold M. (1970) *History of Purple as a Status Symbol in Antiquity*. Latomas Revue D'Etudes Latine, Brussels.

Reinhardt C. and Travis A. S. (2013) *Heinrich Caro and the Creation of the Modern Chemical Industry*. Springer, Dordrecht.

Remy N., Speelman E., and Swartz S. (2016) Style that's sustainable: A new fast-fashion formula. *McKinsey*. https://www.mckinsey.com/capabilities/sustainability/our-insights/style-thats-sustainable-a-new-fast-fashion-formula.

Robson R. (2013) *Dressing Constitutionally: Hierarchy, Sexuality, and Democracy from our Hairstyles to Our Shoes*. Cambridge University Press, Cambridge.

Rocco F. (2010) *The Miraculous Fever-Tree: Malaria, Medicine and the Cure that Changed the World*. Harper Collins, New York, NY.

Rogers Cooper G. (1968) *The Invention of the Sewing Machine*. Smithsonian Institution, Washington, DC.

Romey K. (2016) Was this masterpiece painted with ground mummy? *National Geographic*, 16 September.

Rovine V. L. (2004) Fashionable traditions: the globalization of an African textile. J. Allman (ed.), *Fashioning Africa: Power and the Politics of Dress*. Indiana University Press, Bloomington, IN. pp. 189–211.

Rovine V. L. (2009) Bogolan: *Shaping Culture Through Cloth in Contemporary Mali*. Indiana University Press, Bloomington, IN.

Ruscillo D. (2005) Reconstructing murex royal purple and Biblical blue in the Aegean. In: Bar-Yosef D. (ed.), *Archaeomalacology: Molluscs in Former Environment of Human Behavior*. Oxbow Books, Oxford pp. 99–106.

Russell W. J. (1873) Address to the Chemical Section. *Chemical News and Journal of Science*, 18th September, pp. 148–153.

Sachdev C. (2017) What's making these Dogs in Mumbai turn blue? *NPR*. 26 August.

Salinas M. C. (2017) Mexican cochineal, local technologies and the rise of global trade from the sixteenth to the nineteenth centuries. In: Garcia M. P. and De Sousa L. (eds), *Global History and New Polycentric Approaches: Europe, Asia and the Americas in a World Network System*. Palgrave Macmillan, London, pp. 255–273.

Saltzman M. (1992) Identifying dyes in textiles. *American Scientist* 80(5), pp. 474–481.

Samuel C. (1990) *The Chilkat Dancing Blanket*. University of Oklahoma Press, Norman, OK.

Sanger W. (1858) *A History of Prostitution: Its Extent, Causes, and Effects throughout the world*. Harper and Brothers Publishers, New York.

Santiago E. C. and Meneses Lozano H. M. (2010) Red gold—raising cochineal in Oaxaca. *Textile Society of America Symposium Proceedings*. University of Nebraska, Lincoln, NE.

Schafer E. H. (1956) The Early History of Lead Pigments and Cosmetics in China. *T'oung Pao* 44(4/5), pp. 413–438.

Schmidt H. (1997) Indigo—100 Jahre industrielle Synthese. *Chemie in unserer Zeit* 31(3), pp. 121–128.

Schwarcz J. (2018) Why is there shellac in my chocolate mints? You Asked. McGill Office for Science and Society. https://www.mcgill.ca/oss/article/nutrition-you-asked/why-there-shellac-my-chocolate-mints.

Scientific American. (1871) dyeing turkey red. *Scientific American* 24(4), pp. 57.

Shahid I. (2021) Bioengineered bacteria can make dyes more sustainable. *Massive Science*, 11 June.

Shamas C. (1994) The decline of textile prices in England and America prior to industrialization. *The Economic History Review* 47(3), pp. 483–507.

Shibayama N., Wypyski M., and Gagliardi-Mangilli E. (2015) Analysis of natural dyes and metallic threads used in 16th–18th century Persian/Safavid and Indian/Mughal velvets by HPLC-PDA and SEM-EDS to investigate the system to differentiate velvets of these two cultures. *Heritage Science* 3(12).

Shibayama N., Phipps E., and Commoner L. (2022) Identifying natural dyes to understand a tapestry's origin. The Met. https://www.metmuseum.org/about-the-met/conservation-and-scientific-research/projects/identifying-natural-dyes.

Shively D. H. (1964–1965) Sumptuary regulation and status in early Tokugawa Japan. *Harvard Journal of Asiatic Studies* 25, pp. 123–164.

Shukla P., Upreti D.K., Tiwari P., and Dwivedi A. (2012) Natural thalli and cultured mycobiont of *Usnea ghattensis* G. Awasthi—a potential source of purple dye yielding lichen from India. *Indian Journal of Natural Products and Resources* 3(4), pp. 489–492.

Solly M. (2018) Jerusalem Museum untangles history of the colour blue, from Biblical hue to ancient royalty. *Smithsonian Magazine*, 21 September.

Smith C. S. and Hawthorne J. G. (1974) Mappae Clavicula: a little key to the world of medieval techniques. *Transactions of the American Philosophical Society* 64(4), pp. 1–128.

Smith J. R. (1996) *Safflower*. Taylor and Francis, London.

Srivastaya C. and Bhowmik T. (1968) Lac and paper industry. *Indian Pulp and Paper* 12(8).

Susmann M. (2020) Tyrian, true, royal, or real: archaeological assumptions about the Roman murex dye industry. *Journal of Eastern Mediterranean Archaeology and Heritage Studies* 8(2), pp. 159–173.

Splitstoser J. C., Dillehay T. D., Wouters J., and Claro A. (2016) Early pre-Hispanic use of indigo blue in Peru. *Science Advances* 2(9).

St Clair K. (2016) *The Secret Lives of Colour*. John Murray Press, London.

St Clair K. (2018) *The Golden Thread: How Fabric Changed History*. John Murray Press, London.

Stefanovich O. (2021) Sinixt indigenous nation not 'extinct' in Canada, Supreme Court rules. CBC

News. https://www.cbc.ca/news/canada/british-columbia-sinixt-first-nation-not-extinct-after-all-court-rules-1.4043184.

Steiglitz Robert R. (1994) The Minoan origin of Tyrian purple. *The Biblical Archaeologist* 57(1), pp. 46–54.

Svanberg I. and Ståhlberg S. (2017) Killing wolves with lichens: wolf lichen, *Letharia vulpine* (L.) hue in Scandinavian folk biology. *Swedish Dialects and Folk Traditions*, pp. 173–187.

The Telegraph. (2022) Pictured: piles of Britain's unwanted clothes wash up on Ghana's beaches. *The Telegraph*, 26 July.

Terada T. (2008) Sea snail purple in contemporary Japanese embroidery. *Textile Society of America Symposium Proceedings*. University of Nebraska, Lincoln, NE.

The Guardian (2017) The blue dogs of Mumbai: industrial waste blamed for colourful canines. *The Guardian*, 22 August.

The Morning Chronicle (1851) The Great Exhibition. *The Morning Chronicle*, 17 June, pp. 5.

The New York Times (1898) Weighted silk. *The New York Times*, 2 January, pp. 17.

The New York Times (1972) Era ends: no more black powder at du Pont. *The New York Times*, 7 October, pp. 43, 49.

Theobald M. M. (2012) Putting the red in redcoats. *Colonial Williamsburg Journal, summer*.

Thirsk J. (1997) *Alternative Agriculture: A History from the Black Death to the Present Day*. Oxford University Press, Oxford.

Thurman J. (2003) Mother of invention. *The New Yorker*, 17 October, pp. 58.

Tiffany and Company. (1906) *Dinner in Honor of Sir William Henry Perkin by his American Friends to Commemorate the 50th Anniversary of this Discovery of the Dyestuff Mauve on Saturday, the Sixth of October One Thousand Nine Hundred and Six at Delmonicos*. Tiffany and Co, New York, NY.

Traid (2018) *The Impacts of Clothing Fact Sheets*. Traid, London.

Travis A. S. (1990) Perkin's mauve: ancestor of the organic chemical industry. *Technology and Culture* 31(1), pp. 51–82.

Travis A. S. (1992) August Wilhelm Hofmann (1818–1892). *Endeavour* 16(2), pp. 59–65.

Travis A. (1993) *The Rainbow Makers: The Origins of the Synthetic Dyestuff Industry in Western Europe*. Leigh University Press, Bethlehem.

Travis A. S. (1994) From Manchester to Massachusetts via Mulhouse: the transatlantic voyage of aniline black. *Technology and Culture* 35(1), pp. 70–99.

Travis A. S. (1997) Poisoned groundwater and contaminated soil: the tribulations and trial of the first major manufacturer of aniline dyes in Basel. *Environmental History* 2(3), pp. 343–364

Travis A. S. (2007) Mauve and its anniversaries. *Bulletin of the History of Chemistry* 32(1), pp. 35–44.

Trombert E. (2004) Cooking, dyeing, and worship: the uses of safflower in medieval China as reflected in Dunhuang documents. *Asia Major* 17(1), pp. 59–72.

Turner J. C., Buss E. A., and Mayfield A. E. (2005) Kermes scales (Hemiptera: Kermesidae) on oaks. *Entomology Circular No. 416*. Florida Department of Agriculture and Consumer Services, Division of Plants, Jacksonville, FL.

Turok M. (1988) *El Caracol purpura una tradición milenaria en Oaxaca*. Secretaría de Educación Pública, Dirección General de Culturas Populares, Programa de Artesanías y Culturas Populares, Mexico City.

United Kingdom Parliament (1861) Indigo Planting in Bengal debated on Friday 19 April 1861. *Hansard Report* 162.

United Kingdom Parliament (1993) Harris Tweed Act 1993.

University of Calcutta (1861) Report of the Indigo Commission. 1860. *Calcutta Review* 36, pp. 19–52.

Van Den Belt H. (1992) Why monopoly failed. the rise and fall of Société La Fuschine. *British Journal for the History of Science* 25(1), pp. 45–63.

Vandivere A., Wadum., J., and Leonhardt E. (2020) The girl in the spotlight: Vermeer at work, his materials and techniques in *Girl with a Pearl Earring*. *Heritage Science* 8(20).

Van Zanten V. (2018) Chintz 101: a primer for the print that's back in a big way. *Vogue*, 29 March.

Verberg R. (2018) *Warp-Weighted Loom Weights: Their Story and Use*. Self-published.

Vidyasagar A. (2016) What are lichens? *Live Science*, 8 June.

Wada Y. I. (2002) *Memory on Cloth: Shibori Now*. Kodansha International, Tokyo.

Wada Y. I. (2017) A hidden red. Cooper Hewitt Museum. https://www.cooperhewitt.org/2017/09/17/a-hidden-red/.

Walton Rogers P. (1997) Textile production at 16–22 Coppergate. In: Addyman P.V. (eds) *The Archaeology of York*, vol. 17. *The Small Finds*. Council for British Archaeology, York.

Wang T., Fuller B. T., Jiang H., Li W., Wei D., and Hu Y. (2022) Revealing lost secrets about Yingpan Man and the Silk Road. *Scientific Reports* 12(669).

Watt G. (2014) *A Dictionary of the Economic Products of India*, vol. 4. Gossypium *to* Linociera. Cambridge University Press, Cambridge.

Watts D. C. (2007) *Dictionary of Plant Lore*. Elsevier Science, London.

Wenner N. (2017) *The Production of Indigo Dye from Plants*. Fibershed, San Geronimo, CA.

Weisman S. R. (1987) Many faces of the Mahabharata. *The New York Times*, 27 October.

Wertz J. H., Quye A., France D., Tang P. L., and Richmond L. (2017) Authenticating Turkey red textiles through material investigations by FTIR and UHPLC. *ICOM-CC 18th Triennial Conference Preprints, Copenhagen*.

Westerman A. (2018) Should rivers have same legal rights as humans? A growing number of voices say yes. *NPR*, 3 August.

Wilk S. R. (2021) *Sandbows and Black Light: Reflections on Optics*. Oxford University Press, Oxford.

Wilson H., Carr C., and Hacke M. (2012) Production and validation of model iron-tannate dyed textiles for use as historic textile substitutes in stabilisation treatment studies. *Chemistry Central Journal* 6(1), pp. 44.

Winter J. (2013) *Who Put the Beef Into Wellington?* Kyle Books, London.

Yusuf M (Eds). (2019) *Handbook of Textile Effluent Remediation*. Jenny Stanford Publishing, Singapore.

Wolfe A.J. (2008) Nylon: A revolution in textiles. Science History Institute. https://www.sciencehistory.org/distillations/nylon-a-revolution-in-textiles.

Wong Z. (2017) *Vogue* charts the history of shocking pink. *Vogue*, 28 December.

Wood A. (1856) *A Class-book of Botany Designed for Colleges, Academies and Other Seminaries, in Two Parts*. Crocker and Brewster, Boston, MA.

Woodward C. H. (1949) Vernacular names for *Roccella*. An etymological note. *Bulletin of the Torrey Botanical Club* 76(4), pp. 302–305.

Woytus A. (2017) Synthetic fabrics inspired a cultural revolution. *Jstor Daily*, 19 July.

Wright L. (2017) Kiss me quick: on the naming of commodities in Britain, 1650 to the First World War. In: Wagner E. M., Beinhoff B., and Outhwaite B. (eds), *Merchants of Innovation*. Walter De Gruyter, Boston, MA.

Yang P., Shi W., Wang H., and Liu H. (2016) Screening of freshwater fungi for decolorizing multiple synthetic dyes. *Brazilian Journal of Microbiology* 47(4), pp. 828–834.

Yen Y. L. (2014) Clothing middle-class women: dress, gender and identity in mid-Victorian England c.1850–1875. PhD thesis. University of London, London.

Zapf K. (2020) Some papal bull: 16th century alum trade and English royal autonomy. Summer research. University of Puget Sound, Tacoma.

Index

Image Credits

INTRODUCTION

P. 4 © SLUB / Deutsche Fotothek / Helm, Günther

P. 15 © SLUB / Deutsche Fotothek / Heinrich, Gertrud

P. 19 TOP Photograph by Marli Shamir, 1969, EEPA 2013-009-1188, Marli Shamir Collection, Eliot Elisofon Photographic Archives, National Museum of African Art, Smithsonian Institution BOTTOM Photograph by Marli Shamir, 1969, EEPA 2013-009-1189, Marli Shamir Collection, Eliot Elisofon Photographic Archives, National Museum of African Art, Smithsonian Institution

P. 20 © John Damanti

P. 24 Courtesy of The Book Worm / Alamy Stock Photo

P. 27 Photograph by Robert Ridgway, 1881, SIA RU000095, Smithsonian Institution Archives

P. 31 TOP © Patrick Brown/ Panos Pictures BOTTOM Photograph by Gunnar Sundgren, date unknown, GS11995, Upplandsmuseet's collections, Upplandsmuseet.

P. 33 © Marion Bull / Alamy Stock Photo

P. 38 TOP Photograph by Joseph Bancroft & Sons Co. photographs, Accession 1969.025, 196925_370, Box 3, Folder 3, Audiovisual Collections and Digital Initiatives Department, Hagley Museum and Library, Wilmington, DE 19807 BOTTOM Unknown photographer, c. 1910. Stiftelsen Jamtli

FLORA

P. 45 Workers bringing in and soaking indigo plants, alongside supervisors, at an indigo extraction plant in Szechuan, China, 1929. © SLUB / Deutsche Fotothek /Spainer H

P. 47 *Indigofera tinctoria*, Fabaceae, W 0067742. Natural History Museum, Vienna. www.jacq.org/W0067742

P. 50 TOP © SLUB / Deutsche Fotothek BOTTOM Oscar Mallitte, 1877, ID 189591. Getty Museum Collection. www.getty.edu/art/collection/object/108TA2

P. 55 MeijiShowa / Alamy Stock Photo

P. 59 *Isatis tinctoria* L. 100294715. Hans [Johann] Rudolf Metlesics. Landesmuseums. www.zobodat.at/belege.php?id=100294715

P. 62 TOP Photograph by Sir Rowland Harry Biffen, early 20th century, published in Jamieson Boyd Hurry, *The Woad Plant and its Dye*. Warren Royal Dawson; Oxford University Press, H. Milford, 1930. The Mills Archive Trust BOTTOM © Reginald Wailes/ Anthea de Barton Watson/ The Mills Archive Trust

P. 65 SMK Open, National Gallery of Denmark, KKSgb7480, Statens Museum for Kunst, National Gallery of Denmark

P. 67 *Haematoxylum campechianum* L. 00375616, Percy H. Gentle. National Museum of Natural History. www.si.edu/object/haematoxylum-campechianum-l:nmnhbotany_2520869

P. 71 TOP © Robert Fried / Alamy Banque D'Images BOTTOM Photographer unknown, 1884. IMAGO / Age Photo Stock

P. 75 *Rubia tinctorum* L. 100291316, Hans [Johann] Rudolf Metlesics. Landesmuseums. www.zobodat.at/belege.php?id=100291316

P. 78 Søstrene Persen, 1901. The Fallaize Collection, Wellcome Collection.

P. 87 *Carthamus tinctorius* L. 13045935, Smithsonian National Museum of Natural History. www.si.edu/object/carthamus-tinctorius-l:nmnhbotany_13045935

P. 90 Onono Komachi from the series *Nazorae Rokukasen* (Parodies of the Six Poetic Immortals), Ichiyosai Toyokuni (late Edo Period/latter half of the 19th century). Courtesy of Isehanhonten Co., Ltd

P. 91 ALL Courtesy of Isehanhonten Co., Ltd

P. 93 *Carthamus tinctorius* L. 2014.3012.0012.023, Division of Medicine and Science, National Museum of American History, Smithsonian Institution. www.si.edu/object/carthamus-tinctorius-l-dyers-saffron-safflower:nmah_1459108

P. 97 *Reseda luteola* L. 01205865, Charles Wright, Smithsonian National Museum of Natural History. https://www.si.edu/object/reseda-luteola-l:nmnhbotany_11137300

P. 100 Charles Woolf, ICS12/7503 Weld, 1964 Charles Woolf Slide Collection, Archives & Special Collections, Falmouth University and University of Exeter Penryn Campus © University of Exeter

P. 103 © Arvid Halling Photo Archive /Stiftelsen Jamtli.

FAUNA

P. 107 Murex (*Murex brandaris*), Forbes Pigment Collection, Harvard Art Museums © Pascale Georgiev

P. 109 *Opuntia cochenillifera* L. Decker, B. G. 2230, US National Herbarium Sheet 3723988. Smithsonian National Museum of Natural History. http://n2t.net/ark:/65665/316d2f93a-d5c1-4173-98d3-e34dc5459d18

P. 113 TOP Courtesy of the Trustees of the Natural History Museum, London BOTTOM Theodore Maisch, 1928. Courtesy of Fotos Antiguas Canarias

P. 114 Fotalema Edition, date unknown. Courtesy of Fotos Antiguas Canarias

P. 119 Martin Frobene Ledermuller, Studies of the life cycle of the scale insect Kermes vermilion, *Amusement microscopique, tant pour l'esprit que pour les yeux, contenant ... estampes ... d'apres nature*, Plate 36. Engraved illustration by Adam Wolfgang Winterschmidt, Nuremburg, 1764. © The Royal Society

P. 121 TOP Josephine Powell Slides Collection, © Suna Kıraç Library/Koç University, Turkey BOTTOM Josephine Powell Slides Collection, © Suna Kıraç Library/Koç University, Turkey

P. 124 *The Virgin and Child* (*The Madonna with the Iris*), workshop of Albrecht Dürer, 1500–1510. Courtesy of Bridgeman Images

P. 129 Pieces of stick-lac produced on trees by the lac insect in India © Science Museum Group

P. 133 © TopFoto

P. 137 Murex (*Murex brandaris*), Peter Witte, D-DAI-MAD-WIT-R-216-71-04. Courtesy of Deutsche Archäologische Institut, Madrid

P. 143 Photograph by Alfred Ehrhardt, Murex snail (Stachelschnecke), 1940/41, © Alfred Ehrhardt Stiftung

FUNGI

P. 147 Unknown photographer, Scotland, c. 1920–1930. Courtesy Tasglann nan Eilean

P. 149 *Ochrolechia tartarea* L. 02170718, T. Tønsberg, A Massal, 02170718, Courtesy of the C. V. Starr Virtual Herbarium of The New York Botanical Garden. sweetgum.nybg.org/science/vh

P. 152 Uncredited illustrator, in Johan Peter Westring, *Svenska lafvarnas Färghistoria* (The Dye History of Swedish Lichens), Tryckt hos C. Delén, Stockholm, 1805–[1809]. Plate 15.

P. 153 Uncredited illustrator, in Johan Peter Westring, Svenska lafvarnas Färghistoria (The Dye History of Swedish Lichens), Tryckt hos C. Delén, Stockholm, 1805–[1809]. Plate 13.

P. 157 *Ochrolechia parella* L., A. Massal in GBIF Secretariat, 2022. GBIF Backbone Taxonomy. doi.org/10.15468/39omei

P. 161 *Parmelia saxatilis* L., WU 0041073, F. N. Bornmüller, The Herbarium of the University of Vienna. www.jacq.org/detail.php?ID=1177249

P. 164 © TopFoto / John Topham

P. 165 Courtesy Tasglann nan Eilean

P. 167 © J. L. Rodger. Courtesy Tasglann nan Eilean

P. 169 *Letharia vulpina* L., UC2089693, 051fd9d9-3822-4a18-845b. University of California Berkeley, University Herbarium (UC)

P. 173 © Louis Bockner/ Rossland Museum

P. 175 Fungus (Cortinarius semisanguineus) illustration from *Flora agaricina danica*. Vol. 3-4, Jakob Emanuel Lange, 1938-39. Courtesy of Biblioteca Digital Del Real Jardín Botánico, Madrid, Spain (RJB-CSIC)

P. 179 Courtesy of Felicia Rice and Dorothy M. Beebee

P. 180 © Plantentuin Meise, BE0540708286, Nieuwelaan 18, 1860 Meise

P. 183 TOP Courtesy of Biblioteca Digital Del Real Jardín Botánico, Madrid, Spain (RJB-CSIC) BOTTOM Courtesy of Felicia Rice and Dorothy M. Beebee.

FOSSIL FUELS

P. 186 Cone Mills Dye Lab, North Carolina, 1950s. Courtesy of Arthur d'Arazien Industrial Photographs, Archives Center, National Museum of American History, Smithsonian Institution

P. 189 Dyeing experiments with mauveine on silk by F. E. Meyer, 1925 © Flavia Zumbrunn/ Material Archiv

P. 192 François-Claudins Compte-Calix, engraved by Braequet. Victoria and Albert Museum Department of Prints and Drawings and Department of Paintings Accessions 1957–1958. HMSO, London, 1964. © Victoria and Albert Museum, London

P. 193 TOP © Science Museum / Science & Society Picture Library BOTTOM Courtesy of Division of Medicine and Science, National Museum of American History, Smithsonian Institution

P. 197 Fuchsine crystals at the Bayer Uerdingen, 1965 © Bayer AG, Bayer Archives Leverkusen

P. 201 © Bayer AG, Bayer Archives Leverkusen

P. 204 TOP © Bayer AG, Bayer Archives Leverkusen BOTTOM © Bayer AG, Bayer Archives Leverkusen

P. 207 *Discolorations On Feathers*, a sample book by the Bayer Company, Inc. Date unknown. Courtesy of Science History Institute

P. 210 TOP © Bayer AG, Bayer Archives Leverkusen BOTTOM © Bayer AG, Bayer Archives Leverkusen

P. 213 © Bayer AG, Bayer Archives Leverkusen

P. 215 The aniline colours featured in *Badische Anilin- & Soda-Fabrik*, BASF, 1901. Courtesy of BASF Corporate History

P. 219 Courtesy of *Brooklyn Daily Eagle* photographs, Brooklyn Public Library, Center for Brooklyn History

P. 221 John Vickery, "Indigo," 1937. Courtesy of Science History Institute, Philadelphia

P. 222 TOP Courtesy of BASF Corporate History BOTTOM Courtesy of Science History Institute, Philadelphia

P. 225 © Bayer AG, Bayer Archives Leverkusen

CONCLUSION

P. 227 1972341_0048, DuPont Company Product Information photographs (Accession 1972.341), Audiovisual Collections and Digital Initiatives Department, Hagley Museum and Library, Wilmington, DE 19807. Courtesy of the Hagley Museum and Library

THROUGHOUT

Color wash illustrations by Tegan Hendel, Cæcilie Dyrup and Katty Maurey.

BACK COVER

© TopFoto / John Topham

Acknowledgments

Writing this book has been a wild ride: a deeper, richer, and more challenging experience than I first expected when I enthusiastically (and rather naively) decided to take it on more than two years ago. I'm grateful to everyone who has had a hand in shaping what it's come to be.

Thank you to Morwenna Loughman for feedback on early drafts and to Ananda Pellerin for ping-ponging more iterations of this manuscript back and forth than either of us thought possible. Thank you to Ellie Howard for knowing the visuals that I wanted before I did, and to Tegan Hendel for designing a more beautiful book than I could have imagined. Thank you to my copy-editor and fact checker Nancy Wallace—your attention to detail is infallible (and any errors in this text are entirely my fault). Thank you to Pascale, Kingston, and the team at Atelier Éditions for giving me this opportunity. I am eternally grateful for the chance to share my love of color and dyes (and your seemingly unending patience with me). Thank you to those I spoke to in the process of learning to dye and of writing this book, for giving me your time, your thoughts, and your knowledge: Charllotte Kwon, Amber Muenz, Simone Parrish, Michelle Parrish, Lily Hope, Seathra Bell, Marilyn James, Taress Alexis, Kathryn Davey, Clare Johnston, Dorothy Beebee, Felicia Rice, Mouhamad Ghassen Nouira, Suzanne Kuechler, Zenzie Tinker Conservation (and her very accommodating staff), and many others.

Thank you to my parents, Jan Brown and Hugh MacDonald, for supporting my curiosity and eccentric hobbies from the very beginning, and for their ongoing encouragement (and to my siblings, Isaac and Skye, for the same). Thank you to Alice Costelloe for taking me for walks and letting me bounce ideas. Thank you to Aaron Gasparik for your library card. Thank you to everyone, at every party/barbecue/dinner/social event over the years who has listened patiently as my rants about cochineal stretch on longer than any human can be reasonably expected to stay interested. And finally, the biggest thank you to my partner, William Jack, for bringing me endless cups of black coffee, listening to me read the same passages aloud approximately 1,200 times, having the utmost faith me, and pushing me to finish what I start. I love you and am forever grateful.

Lauren MacDonald is a multidisciplinary designer, researcher, and founder of the textiles studio Working Cloth. She has a background in material culture, textile science, and fashion.

Author. Lauren MacDonald
Editorial director. Pascale Georgiev
Managing editor. Lucy Kingett
Editor. Ananda Pellerin
Copy-editor. Nancy Wallace
Proofreader. Helius
Indexer. Annette Musker
Design. Tegan Ella Hendel
Picture research. Ellie Howard

atelier éditions | d·a·p

First edition of 4,500
Printed in Italy on 100% ecological paper from sustainable forests
978-1-954957-00-8

Published by
Atelier Éditions
Los Angeles, USA
www.atelier-editions.com

Co-Published and Distributed by
D.A.P./Distributed Art Publishers
75 Broad Street
Suite 630
New York, NY 10004
www.artbook.com